MW01711732

PERSEVERANCE

THE STORY OF CAPE BRETON'S UNIVERSITY COLLEGE
1952-2002

BY
ROBERT MORGAN

UNIVERSITY COLLEGE OF CAPE BRETON PRESS
SYDNEY, NOVA SCOTIA

Book layout by Gail Jones, UCCB Press, Sydney, NS.
Cover Design by Brennan MacDonald, Glace Bay, NS.
Printed and bound by Kromar, Winnipeg, MA

National Library of Canada Cataloguing in Publication

Morgan, Robert J.
Perseverance: the story of Cape Breton's University College, 1952-2002 / Robert J. Morgan.

Includes bibliographical references and index.
ISBN 0-920336-99-X

1. University College of Cape Breton—History. I. Title.

LE3.C326M67 2004 378.716'95 C2004-902021-8

University College of Cape Breton Press Inc.
P.O. Box 5300
Sydney, Nova Scotia
B1P 6L2

www.uccbpress.ca

TABLE OF CONTENTS

List of photographs and credits

Acknowledgements

I would like to thank those who helped me prepare the manuscript for this book. Special thanks to Anne Connell, Anne Michele Chiasson, and Philomena Sutherland, who guided me through the pitfalls of computer use.

The staff of the president's office were also very kind and helpful, particularly Deborah George and Lynda Moffatt. Likewise, Catherine MacKenzie at the St. FX archives made my task much easier.

I would like to acknowledge and thank faculty and staff of UCCB, especially those cited in the bibliography, for their helpful information and forthright opinions.

Finally, thanks to UCCB Press, both for their thoughtful comments and for their commitment to the University College and to Silver Donald Cameron for his comments and kind words.

FOREWORD

THE UNIVERSITY COLLEGE OF THE FUTURE*

by Silver Donald Cameron

In 1824, the "leading men of Sydney" tried to establish an institution of higher education in Cape Breton. It took them 150 years—and the College of Cape Breton established in 1974 was still not a fully-independent institution. Until it metamorphosed into the University College of Cape Breton in 1982, its degrees were officially conferred by St. Francis Xavier University.

The Story of Cape Breton's University College is the fierce struggle of Cape Bretoners for their own unique institution, despite relentless opposition from the mainland. Nova Scotia has always had innumerable degree-granting colleges and universities elsewhere, half-a-dozen in Halifax alone. But Cape Breton, with 20 percent of the province's population, including its second-largest urban centre, had none at all.

Cape Breton, of course, has always been the wrong side of Nova Scotia's tracks: blue-collar, polyglot, leftist, irreverent, and sweaty. In the early 20th century, steel-milling Sydney and its coal-mining neighbours constituted the engine which drove the whole Maritime economy. The area attracted workers from around the world: Ukrainians, Scots, Poles, Newfoundlanders, Italians, Jews, West Indians, Lebanese. Facing appalling working conditions, Cape Breton's workers organized militant, fearless unions. They elected Communist mayors and CCF MPs, flew the red flag in May Day parades, and survived depressions and lock-outs with stolen coal, kitchen gardens, codfish and moonshine.

---

* A version of this foreword has also appeared in the Sunday Herald, Halifax, NS (18 April, 2004).

Their defiance scared the muttonchops off Halifax. Give those barbarians a university? Grudgingly, at best. The new college, Morgan notes, "was not allowed to offer programs duplicating those of other universities." All new programs needed external approval, and the authorities took 14 years to approve its BSc in Nursing.

The need to innovate marked UCCB from the start. As a "university college," created by merging a junior college and a trades-training institute, it strove to integrate trades and technology programs with academic degrees—with some success. A UCCB student can take a two-year co-op technology diploma, transfer to a degree program, and emerge with vocational training, an academic credential (and little debt) in little longer than the time usually required simply to obtain a degree. But just when UCCB's faculty were proposing a range of innovative programs, governments were cutting university funding across the board. In effect, government had required UCCB to develop novel programs, and then declined to finance them. When I was a dean there, ten years ago, UCCB was Canada's worst-funded university by far.

Yet Cape Breton's desperate need for higher education had already made UCCB one of Nova Scotia's larger universities, with more than 3800 students packed into buildings designed for 1200. About 80 percent of the students had loans, as opposed to 20 percent elsewhere. I remember students so poor that they ate from food banks and slept in their cars. UCCB grew by building partnerships with Enterprise Cape Breton Corporation, the Fortress of Louisbourg National Historic Park, the Canadian Coast Guard College and the Gaelic College of Celtic Arts and Crafts. It offered the first "process education" degree in Canada, the Bachelor of Arts Community Studies (BACS). It soon added the BA, BSc and BBA degrees as well as the only Bachelor of Technology east of Toronto. It now offers six forms of B.Tech, two innovative Master's degrees, and a Bachelor of Science Community Studies which incorporates traditional knowledge, notably from the Mi'kmaq culture.

Always close to its community, UCCB attracted the largest contingent of native students in the Maritimes, created a new curriculum in Mi'kmaq

Studies, and became Atlantic Canada's recognized leader in coop education. It developed a CAD/CAM Centre, a Geographical Information Systems Centre and an Environmental Services Lab serving local industrial and governmental clients. The SSHRC and NSERC awarded it a Chair in the Management of Technological Change, which led to a monthly meeting of a Technology Advisory Group of researchers, entrepreneurs, investors, civil servants. The TAG was largely responsible for the emergence of a high-tech industry in Sydney.

Constantly striving to do more than it could afford, UCCB was often a tumultuous place. At one point, it was carrying a $3.5 million debt—and facing further cutbacks. In a three-year period, it cycled and recycled five presidents, two of them "Acting." One was fired, and then reinstated after suing successfully for wrongful dismissal. The institution endured a faculty strike and three more presidents within the following decade. And yet, in 1994, when Maclean's magazine made a rare attempt to assess "value-added"—not the size of the library or the endowment, but the actual benefits which universities confer on their students—gritty, impoverished UCCB led the nation. What Bob Morgan calls "enforced creativity" may be the very thing that caused UCCB to blossom. Determined to succeed against all odds, UCCB has developed a unique capacity to serve the real needs of a 21st-Century post-industrial community. Rooted, pragmatic, nimble and adventurous, it may just be the university of the future.

Silver Donald Cameron, April 2004

INTRODUCTION

The history of most universities is not written until they have endured for many years. Yet the University College of Cape Breton has developed so rapidly, is changing so quickly and is such an unusual institution, the author has felt that its history should be communicated while many of its founders are still alive.

The development of higher education in Cape Breton Island is largely the story of the pursuit of a vision which has persisted over 150 years. It is the concept of an institution grounded in its community, combining all aspects of learning: academic, technological, and mechanical.

In writing this history, the author has had the two-fold task of tracing the quest of this vision while telling the factual story of the place.

It is hoped that this book will help readers understand what this university stands for and serve as an informative handbook outlining steps in the evolution of various sectors of the institution.

This book is dedicated to all those who have contributed so much of their lives toward the development of this unique university.

I

The Vision of the Founders

The idea of establishing a post-secondary educational institution in Cape Breton was an old one. The concept always emphasized the practical training of people for the good of the community so that they could better earn a living. So-called higher learning was sometimes thought of, but the element of practical training was always there.

That notion sprang from early nineteenth-century precedents, when, in 1824, the swelling population of Scottish setters on the island led Father William B. MacLeod to begin a school at East Bay, known as "the College," for the training of priests. He was supported by several "leading men of Sydney," including "Dodd" (likely Murray Dodd, MLA), and High Sheriff, C.E. Leonard, neither of whom was Roman Catholic, but who obviously saw the practical benefits of attending to the needs of the settlers.[1] The college at East Bay was considered too far from the centres of population and when Cape Breton came under the jurisdiction of the

Diocese of Nova Scotia, it was closed around 1830 and an Academy was established in the more populous and centrally located Arichat with the same aims as the East Bay school.[2] That Academy ceased to exist in 1841.

After the Diocese of Nova Scotia was divided in two in 1844, the busy port of Arichat, on Isle Madame, became the seat of the new diocese. Bishop Colin MacKinnon, worked to have the annual grant to the Academy restored and, in July 1853, the former Academy was reopened and renamed "St. Francis Xavier's College." MacKinnon however, favoured a college in his native Antigonish where his predecessor had established a school in 1829, and by 1854, he was building "an Academy" there. [3] Both institutions operated at the same time, Arichat was assigned the lower grades and called "Arichat Academy;" Antigonish Academy, the "public school," became "St. Francis Xavier's College." In 1855 the students and the seminarians of college rank were all transferred from Arichat to Antigonish.[4] Meanwhile, at the other end of Cape Breton Island, Sydney got an academy (1841), but after 1855 neither lay nor clerical students could obtain higher education on Cape Breton.

With the centres of speculative learning removed first to Arichat and finally to the mainland, education in the Sydney area took on a more practical function. This was evidenced during the late 1830s, when a Mechanics Institute was established there, sponsoring lectures on practical and philosophical topics. In 1845, a Sydney Scientific and Literary Society began with a lecture on the science of electricity to raise funds to purchase "philosophical apparatus for the benefit of society."[5] Without government or religious support to institutionalize them, these private efforts didn't last because the small population of the area could not justify the investment.

At the end of the 19th century, the rapid growth of the coal industry and the erection of the steel plant changed the situation. In 1905, Dalhousie University, seeing the possibilities of expanding into the rapidly growing industrial area, set out to establish a "first class mechanics' school" in Sydney. The plan was for students to study at this evening school and then to enter King's School of Engineering in Halifax, so that the two institutions would complement each other.[6] The plan failed to receive support or funding, but the idea of some kind of institution for the practical training of workers arose again in 1921, when the convention of the Independent Labour Party of Nova Scotia endorsed the idea of a labour college in Sydney. Professors would be hired to teach engineering, mathematics and economics. Local members of the party would pledge $2.00 per month for the payment of the professors.[7] Unfortunately the Labour Party never came to power and this idea died as well.

The Great Depression also contributed to the need for a post-secondary educational institution in Cape Breton. Travelling for education in those years was beyond the means of most people. In 1931 mining school classes were delivered in Glace Bay to teach electrical engineering, mechanical drawing, and steam engineering so that men could qualify for senior positions up to that of mines manager.[8] By 1937, people were calling for a community college in Cape Breton which would teach the first two years of university thus opening the door for pupils to professional schools on the mainland. One writer to the *Sydney Post* implored that the institution should not be a college in the narrowest sense, but a centre for community welfare for the "spiritual, mental, and physical uplift of our people."[9] This new idea seemed to strike a popular note, blending vocational, academic and community elements in one institution.

This ferment led a group of community leaders in the industrial community to consider more seriously the idea of some form of higher education in the area. In 1938, their leaders, D.S. Morrison, a member of the United Church, and Father Thomas O'Reilly Boyle investigated such a proposal. Morrison was an engineer employed by the Dominion Steel Company and various towns in the industrial area. Boyle, formerly of Saint Francis Xavier University (St. FX), but stationed in New Waterford, had urged that university form an extension department in the 1920s.[10] Morrison and Boyle met with the Reverend "Jimmy" Tompkins, outspoken parish priest at Reserve Mines and a well-known social activist. They also sought the assistance of George Morrison, MLA for Sydney to bring their cause before government. In March, 1938, D.S. Morrison wrote to George Morrison:

> Speaking, as you would be, on behalf of some 100,000 people located in this immediate vicinity, and who supply such a large percentage of the revenue of the Province, who are now without any greater educational advantages than are enjoyed at Ingonish (or very nearly as bad as that), I feel that you would have no trouble in convincing your leaders that we have a good case.[11]

Morrison's plan was to have the MLA press H.P. Moffatt, a former teacher at Sydney Academy and at that time head of the research branch of the Nova Scotia Department of Education, to study the situation in the industrial area and to find educational models in areas of the United States that were suffering similar disadvantages. Morrison anticipated the objections that other colleges would make toward another such an establishment in Sydney but brushed them aside, writing: "Not only would they get more students from this section but they would be advanced students, old enough to know what they are after and not liable to compel professors to waste time on elementary subjects."[12] George Morrison contacted the Department of Education, but D. S. Morrison had little faith in the bureaucrats, urging Boyle to have "all our guns and ammunition in readiness to take the initiative...."[13] He asked Boyle to champion the cause and to prepare a written "Case for a Junior College in Cape Breton."[14] However, Boyle's effectiveness was impaired by the continued displays of public drunkenness that had caused his dismissal from St. FX. As well, his left-leaning politics hardly endeared him to Nova Scotia politicians.[15]

The first round in the battle for a college in Sydney was won by the St. FX Extension Department. This department had been established by Reverend Moses Coady[16] in 1928, in answer to the growing social and economic problems facing the people of eastern Nova Scotia, as well as the fear of political radicalism, especially communism, that was gaining a foothold in industrial Cape Breton. A series of rural conferences were held, mainly at St. FX, with clerical leaders Boyle and Tompkins using them to advance their reformist ideas. In 1930, the Extension Department came up with a blueprint to train farmers, fishermen, and lumbermen how to solve their own economic and social problems. Correspondence courses, study clubs, radio courses, and night schools were held in the region. In 1932 extension offices were opened in Glace Bay and credit unions soon followed. The 1930s were indeed the "glory days" of St. FX Extension. The appeal of radicals was diminished and by the end of the 1930s Coady felt the extension movement had "licked them." The Extension Department altered the character of St. FX, pushing it beyond its earlier emphasis on classical and professional higher education into mass adult education.[17] It made education more relevant to people in industrial Cape Breton and quelled calls for a local college.

An even stronger force than the efforts to make St. FX more attractive halted moves for better educational opportunities in Cape Breton: World War Two. Resources were poured into the victory effort and in 1941 the Extension Department closed its Glace Bay office in an attempt to reduce expenditures.[18] In the long run, however, the war nurtured the growing technological revolution which demanded skilled technicians and engineers. St. FX, which had channeled its practical educational efforts into the Extension Department, now began to incorporate utilitarian studies into its curriculum. This sparked fiery opposition from those advocating the university's traditional denominational aims and emphasis on liberal arts. The situation heated up with the appointment of Dr. Patrick J. Nicholson as president in 1944. A traditionalist, he saw education as "preparation for complete living" and the university primarily as a minor seminary.[19]

The people in industrial Cape Breton, however, had more practical things on their minds, including the expense of getting any kind of higher education. In 1949, three out of every four students from the Diocese of Antigonish attending St. FX were from Cape Breton, with those from the industrial area making seventy percent of that number.[20] Tuition and residency fees in 1938 were $342, a huge amount of money at the time.[21] Reverend Boyle and his supporters, after the wartime lapse, again called for a junior college, pointing out that by 1947, student fees at a typical mainland university amounted to only $188, but residential or boarding costs drove up costs to Cape Bretoners. A student living within reach of a college would pay the $188, while a typical student from Cape Breton paying residential or boarding costs would pay $513.[22] While studying at home also cost money, it certainly did not as seriously impinge upon the family budget as studying away from home. Boyle calculated that tuition for a locally based college would amount to roughly $160 per year.

The kind of institution Boyle envisaged was a junior college capable of teaching the three years following matriculation. A university was out of the question since the area did not have the population to support such an institution. He estimated that there were 500 Cape Bretoners of college status studying in mainland universities; with an enrolment of 200 students and 10 faculty, a local college could have an annual revenue of $35,000 with salaries amounting to $40,000; with 300 students, tuition would cover costs of teaching and leave a margin for laboratory costs and office expenses. Later, as enrolment increased, the fees could be lowered.

Capital costs were another matter. Boyle advocated renting Sydney Academy high school classrooms after regular classes from 4 to 9 p.m. and all day Saturday. He felt this arrangement ideal since it allowed working people to take classes, thereby paying their own way. As for laboratories and library, a wooden building of "cheap, army style construction" could be erected nearby to serve temporarily until a new vocational school, which he hoped to see erected, could house such facilities. The building and books for the library would require but a small capital expenditure, and he advocated that endowment funds be sought immediately.

The junior college would offer the same courses as other Maritime colleges during the three years following Grade 11. At the time, Grade 12 in the Maritimes was identical to first year college, graduates of Grade 12 would enter as sophomores. Freshmen classes would be available for Grade 11 graduates, for repeaters, for the employed returning to study, for war veterans, and in special cases for regular high school students.[23] There was no debate as to the utility of the studies to be offered. As well as traditional courses in arts and science, it would offer preparation for professional schools, for occupations requiring study beyond the high school level, and maybe even fit into the provincial normal school system for training teachers.

When it came to the question of ownership and control of such an institution, Boyle felt that the province's system of colleges, maintained by churches at great financial sacrifice, while fine for character building when students were far from home, would be impractical locally. Not only would students be living under parental authority, but also each denomination could appoint a clergyman who would be chaplain and professor of religion for his group. Institutional ownership would be vested in a Board of Trustees composed of representatives appointed by local governments and by Acadia, Dalhousie, Mount Allison and St. Francis Xavier universities on the Mainland.

Boyle was breaking with tradition in an attempt to mobilize local support for a junior college. He was not giving St. FX, his former employer, any privileged place in higher education in Cape Breton and he wasn't concerned with the debate between useful and theoretical education, or the preparation of men for the priesthood. Boyle envisioned a utilitarian, non-denominational college that would reflect the unique multicultural character of Cape Breton. Only the "united, democratic action of our ordinary citizens" could bring this about.[24]

The location of a junior college in Sydney was of great concern to St. Francis Xavier University. With the population of Industrial Cape Breton expanding rapidly in the early years of the twentieth century, there was a growing realization of the anomaly that in the diocese the bishop's residence, the cathedral and the university were located 200 kilometres from the bulk of the population. There was a real fear that the university might be transferred to Sydney until the first stone structure, Morrison Hall, was erected at the Antigonish campus in 1938; the permanence of the Antigonish university was thus cast in stone. The status quo could not be maintained, however. Rumours were rife that another university, likely Dalhousie, had obtained an option on land within Sydney for future expansion.[25]

These rumours and the timely appointment of Rev. John R. MacDonald as Bishop of Antigonish, in June 1950, finally made the dream of a local college a reality. A native of Port Hood, he had already gained a reputation for his administrative abilities, as well as his interest in social advancement.[26] In his earlier days, he was deeply involved in the establishment of the Extension Department of St. FX and was keenly aware of the educational needs of working-class people in his diocese. A man capable of "razor sharp analysis," he quickly perceived the "seething sense of neglect among the people in the [industrial] part of his diocese, where there was clearly a serious need for improved opportunity for youth in search of higher education."[27] MacDonald's interest in education was clearly shown in his previous attempt to establish technical schools for boys in New Glasgow and Sydney. He hoped to open the first of these in Sydney, and had discussed the plan with laymen and priests there. He was disappointed that both groups felt that the province—and not the Church—should build such a school.[28]

The establishment of a college as part of St. FX was different in that higher education in Nova Scotia was still largely under the auspices of religious denominations, with very little government assistance.[29] Money was not easy to come by, and even the maintenance of the University's Extension Department in a Sydney warehouse was difficult to finance. With the fear of Dalhousie establishing a feeder college in Sydney, MacDonald had to find a way of quickly establishing a college in Sydney with just the financial support of the Church, St. FX and particularly its more affluent supporters in the industrial area.

Within five months of his appointment as bishop, MacDonald formulated his strategy and, on a dreary evening, in November 1950, he invited two St. FX administrators, Rev. Dr. Malcolm Angus MacLellan, Dean of Studies, and Rev. Hugh J. Somers, Director of Finance to his residence.[30] These three men of very different temperaments, two of them Cape Bretoners, laid the groundwork for the new college.

The Bishop told them that he was convinced that St. FX must open a junior college in Sydney. Both men agreed, but all three realized the greatest challenge was financing, and only a powerful body like the Catholic Church, which could count on the services of priests and voluntary contributions from the community, could operate such a body.[31] The agreement spurred Bishop MacDonald to bring the matter before the President, P. J Nicholson, who in turn presented the proposal for a junior college to the University's Board of Governors, on January 8, 1951.[32] At the meeting, the university administration was authorized to investigate the feasibility of setting up the college to give courses at the sophomore level. A joint committee representing the board and university council was appointed to proceed with the project.[33]

After engineering this move, with his usual dispatch MacDonald headed for Sydney where, he had learned, Sacred Heart Parish in the city's north end was having difficulties in maintaining its parish centre, the old Lyceum Building. The Lyceum had been built in 1904 as an educational, social, and theatrical centre and had rapidly become a popular locale for plays, shows and vaudeville, attracting top flight performers in the early years of the century. When the advent of movies and radio threatened its existence, it eventually became a financial drain on the parish. It was a solidly built four-storey structure with walls nearly a metre thick in places, a basement with a gymnasium, and an upper storey with club rooms and a library. Interestingly, the building had always been seen as a cultural centre and the very name "Lyceum," named for the garden in which Aristotle taught, translates as "a teaching place."[34]

MacDonald brought the joint committee to Sacred Heart Glebe House, next door to the Lyceum, on January 24, 1951 and called the parish priest, Monsignor R.C. MacGillivray, to be present. MacLellan and Somers had produced a report on the college for the meeting, which became the guidelines for the proposed institution. It was agreed that the college would open in September of that year in the Lyceum, which following alterations and repairs, would be deeded to the university by the parish.

The subordinate role of the college as an adjunct and feeder to St. Francis Xavier University was emphasized from day one by the adoption of the name "Xavier Junior College." The powers of the head of the institution, known as the "Principal," were restricted. He or she would be responsible for scholastic and financial administration of the Junior College, but would report to the parent institution. He or she could recommend staff appointments, but this had to be confirmed by the University Council. All important expenditures had to receive the approval of the Board of Governors. The approval of Council was required in all major scholastic matters and regular reports were to be made to the Board of Governors. As far as capital expenditures, the authority of the University's signing officers was needed for all significant expenditures.

As a further restriction, the Junior College was not to enter into competition with existing educational facilities in the area.[35] This was meant to allay the fears of business and secretarial schools, and to prevent any active competition for Grade 11 graduates from high schools.

Bishop MacDonald's next important step was to appoint a principal. He chose Malcolm MacLellan who, along with H.J. Somers, had been a right-hand man in establishing the Junior College. Shortly after the meeting in Sydney, MacDonald met MacLellan on the campus at St. FX, and in the casual way that foreshadowed later Junior College appointments, put the proposition to him.[36] On the surface the appointment was logical. MacLellan was forty-four and a Cape Bretoner who, among many other things, was proving his mettle in positions such as Dean of Studies, advisor to the Minister of Education and Chairman of the Antigonish County School Board. He was affable, efficient, serious, and a dedicated son of the university.

MacLellan professed to be "stunned" by the proposition since he had not given it much thought.[37] He was filled with feelings of inadequacy: he was not adventuresome enough; he suffered from pernicious anemia; how could he face the thought of leaving the peaceful, established rural campus to establish a little college in a converted vaudeville theatre in an industrial city already facing serious economic challenges? He was also mildly disappointed to learn that he was not indispensable to the university in his present positions.[38]

On the other hand, there was no turning down Bishop "John. R." MacLellan was a loyal priest and Xaverian who was obedient to, and admiring of, his bishop. This is not to say he did not advise alternatives. Why not, for example, choose H.J. Somers, the bishop's other chief mentor in the project? MacLellan consulted President Nicholson on this point. Nicholson bluntly informed him that he needed Somers for fundraising at St. FX and did not want him involved "in less important business like Xavier Junior College."[39] MacLellan, his ego slightly bruised, had no alternative but to take on the job and by February, 1951, his appointment was announced.

If MacLellan accepted the position reluctantly, he pursued it with single-mindedness, deep involvement and a conscientiousness that left an indelible mark on the character of the Junior College. He eagerly drove to Sydney to inspect his new college building but was distressed by what he found there. How could he possibly convert what was basically a "useless" four-storey, thousand-seat theatre into an academic building?[40] He and other members of the joint committee met with builders who estimated that it would cost only $25,000 to repair the basement and fourth floors in time for a September opening. MacLellan, though still dejected by the building's inadequacy, authorized the repairs and headed back to Antigonish to prepare for his move to Sydney and the Sacred Heart Glebe House.

A short while after his arrival, on the morning of March 7,1951, he was awakened by a Sister of St. Martha, who exclaimed, "Father, your college burned down last night!"[41] MacLellan experienced a surge of sensations:

> It was definitely a shocking surprise and despite that reaction, I felt myself experiencing a sensation of relief, a burden seemed to be lifting off my mind. Immediately, I thought, maybe now the whole thing is off, or at least postponed indefinitely.[42]

A twenty-seven-year-old plasterer's apprentice had gone on a rampage in the early hours of the morning, setting fire to three buildings in Sydney, including the Lyceum, while setting off false alarms to delay the firemen. By morning the building was a smoldering ruin, with only the thick walls standing. Damage was estimated at $250,000. Fortunately, work had not yet begun on the building. Ironically, the specifications had been mailed to Antigonish the evening before the fire.[43]

Three days later, MacLellan and the other members of the joint committee met with the Bishop at Sacred Heart Rectory. With the future of the college in trouble, Monsignor MacGillivray of Sacred Heart offered $50,000 insurance money for the Lyceum to the university, if the building were reconstructed. Other members of the committee now favoured Moxham's Castle, a massive turn-of-the-century home of an early general manager of the Sydney Steel Plant, which was for sale for $100,000. The committee immediately decided to inspect the site, which extended 300 metres along Sydney's King's Road and stretched to the waterfront. MacLellan was very much taken with it, but the Bishop decreed that it was too grandiose for use as a college. As MacLellan rephrased it, "it was too nice to have it opened to a crowd of unruly students."[44] There was no debate and the restoration of the Lyceum carried the day.

As the cleanup of the Lyceum began, it became all too obvious that costs for the reconstruction of the building were going to be a great deal higher than earlier predicted. Where was the extra money going to come from? A fundraising committee was organized, with MacLellan at the fore, to solicit donations from local business and union leaders of all religious stripes, but the result was a great disappointment. Still commuting between Antigonish and Sydney, MacLellan was unfamiliar with the industrial area of Cape Breton; he knew nothing of the internal social and personal relationships of the community and had to rely on local Catholic clergy for contacts. Among the clergy and others there were conflicting views as to whether the Lyceum was an appropriate location. Seeing the split in the community, the manager of the Steel Plant, Lionel A. Forsyth refused to co-operate. Other business leaders simply did not answer MacLellan's calls, pleaded pressing financial needs of other projects, or stayed loyal to other universities. After ten days of this MacLellan was in a "confused state."[45]

With the Bishop and President threatening to end the project unless local money were found, MacLellan decided he needed to live in Sydney so he moved into Sacred Heart Rectory. The rector, Monsignor MacGillivray, convinced him to take the $50,000 Lyceum insurance money and use it as the basis for the $85,000 he must raise to restore the Lyceum to a three-storey structure. Carpenters were hired and work began in May with the job to be completed by September 15. Always able to look on the brighter side of things, MacLellan reflected that the Lyceum fire had been a blessing in disguise—it allowed him to transform the building into a more suitable academic structure.[46]

Nevertheless, problems continued to mount. He had to hire a staff and find a residence to house the priests who would make up a large portion of the faculty. A residence was acquired when MacLellan convinced the university to purchase the spacious Charles Wilson residence in nearby Westmount for $16,000. Then, as he supervised work on the Lyceum and modifications to the Wilson House, he began hiring staff. Fortunately, his academic contacts were better than his business and labour contacts and he recruited a multi-talented staff. He relied on St. FX staff where available, like Reverend Frank Smythe who was happy to teach economics, sociology, and religion—then a requirement for Catholic students.

When informed by the Bishop that he could hire a diocesan priest, MacLellan immediately lit upon a fellow Invernesser, Reverend Charles W. MacDonald, "an intelligent and progressive person" to teach philosophy, Latin and religion.[47] Father MacDonald ("Father Charlie," or "Charlie *beag*")[48] was a brilliant choice; his humanity, courage and insight would contribute immeasurably to the character and development of the institution. MacDonald, Smythe and MacLellan formed a triumvirate that guided the college through its early years.

For English and French, MacLellan relied on Yves Brunelle, a bilingual former student who was working on his doctorate at the University of Michigan, at an annual salary of $2,800. He also needed a "relatively versatile" science teacher, and Elmer Britten agreed to teach first-year chemistry and mathematics. He got a young lawyer, Robert S. MacLellan, to teach history, Ann Terry MacLellan, highly regarded as the region's most brilliant elocutionist, to teach public speaking, and Marie LeBlanc, later Superior-General of the Sisters of St. Martha, to teach preparatory French.[49] MacLellan himself would conduct psychology and religion classes.

Academic progress was not matched on the construction front, unfortunately. In early May the local Carpenter's Union went on strike and work on the Lyceum stopped. The strike dragged on most of the summer and MacLellan could see that the building would not be ready by September. A frantic search for temporary quarters led him to a location across George Street from the Lyceum. One of the temporary wooden Navy League Huts built for the entertainment of sailors during the War had been left standing for Sea Cadet gatherings.[50] The directors of the building allowed the college to use one of the buildings as its first home. "I doubt," wrote MacLellan, "if any institution of higher learning ever started in such unpretentious conditions."[51]

With a building of sorts and staff in hand, a serious search for students could now begin, and this is where MacLellan truly shone. He beat a path to every Roman Catholic pastor in the area cajoling them to use their considerable influence to encourage students to attend the college. Just as important, especially in the enrolment of those of other faiths, was a positive relationship with the high school principals, particularly the venerable Sydney Academy. George G. Campbell, a far-seeing history scholar though not of the Catholic faith, swung his support behind the new institution, helping to overcome the religious barriers of the period and launching the institution on its path of religious diversity.

As summer approached, matters began to improve. By June, the Navy League Hut was being prepared for classrooms. The carpenter's strike finally ended in September and the first student registrations were being received at MacLellan's temporary headquarters in the Sacred Heart Rectory. In August, MacLellan moved his office into the cramped Navy

League Building and, by early September, Fathers C.W. MacDonald and Frank Smythe had moved into the unfinished Westmount Residence.

On September 17, 1951, Xavier Junior College convened its first classes. Sixty full-time students were joined by 85 part-time, most of whom were teachers-in-service. Eight courses were provided for teachers and 20 for full-time students, ranging from college preparatory to the sophomore level. MacLellan undoubtedly marvelled at the miracle that had brought the college that far when Mass for faculty and students was celebrated a few days later at Sacred Heart Church, in keeping with the Catholic tradition of the university.

Yet the celebration was premature. Eight days later the Westmount residence caught fire. Shocked and sick to his stomach, MacLellan rushed to the scene to witness flames shooting from the roof and firemen scrambling to gain control of the blaze. The painters had used a blowtorch to burn away the paint from the building's exterior and the flame had penetrated the dry wall. The fire was extinguished after about two hours, but the building was seriously damaged and the priests had to move into Sacred Heart Rectory until their residence, which was insured, was repaired, though not until the following January.[52]

Fig. 1. Photo of staff and regular students, first year at Xavier Junior College in Navy League Building. Staff: Rev. C.W. MacDonald, Yves Brunelle, Rev. M. MacLellan, Elmer Britten, Jean MacPhee, F.J. Smythe. 1951. Beaton Institute of Cape Breton Studies, University College of Cape Breton. 80-160-434.

Against the odds, it seemed, the Lyceum was also ready for occupancy in January. The local press was duly impressed by the new quarters:

> On the basement floor separate lounges have been provided for the boys and girls and ... individual lockers for students where outdoor clothing and student belongings are kept.... Four spacious classrooms opening off a wide hall share the second floor with a compact administration section which contains offices and a staff room.
>
> A modern and well-quipped science laboratory is located on the basement floor and four modern washrooms complete with showers made (sic) up sanitary facilities.
>
> New quarters for the Extension Department ... have been provided in the building with the offices and a conference room, also located on the ground floor.
>
> The highlight of the rebuilding program, however, is to be found on the top floor which is given over almost entirely to a spacious auditorium which will also do duty as a study hall, library and headquarters for large-group extension work, study and lectures.[53]

Five hundred people crammed into the top floor auditorium for the Grand Opening, January 16, 1952. The Bishop, administrators of St. FX, school officials, and Principal MacLellan gave and heard numerous speeches. Two particularly prophetic notes were struck. Thomas L. Sullivan, Supervisor of Schools for Cape Breton, who delivered the principal address, spoke of the institution exploring new methods and fields of endeavour.[54] Rev. Moses Coady, a Cape Bretoner and insightful founder of the University's Extension Department, wired a message saying "the past history of Cape Breton is proof that people of many races and cultures can come together for the development of a free industrial society.... The founding of Xavier College (sic) presages a new era in the flowering of that life and civilization."[55] The building of a multi-cultural institution exploring new fields and methods of learning was a challenge that the little college would have to meet if it was to survive.

II

The MacLellan Era, 1952-1965

Malcolm MacLellan brought a definite philosophy of education to Xavier Junior College, or XJC as it was fondly known. (The institution was also sometimes referred to locally as "little X.") His concepts formed the basis of the institution's philosophy for the first decades of its existence, part of the bedrock of its principles.

MacLellan believed deeply that the only reliable basis for an education system is a philosophy that seeks the "lasting qualities of life;" education methods might change, but the old values, based largely on Catholic philosophy, should remain.[1] This led to a hierarchical view of knowledge that placed philosophy and theology that dealt with "higher ideals," above science which "can never determine the purpose of our life, nor can it be that purpose."[2] His own education had exposed him to the concept of junior colleges, two-year institutions becoming popular in the United

Fig. 2. Xavier Junior College, c1950. Beaton Institute of Cape Breton Studies, University College of Cape Breton. 83-6563-13863.

States where he had studied. He believed some people need only obtain a few years of college for career development and felt strongly that a junior college should be a "local institution to make its opportunities available to all."[3] These concepts dovetailed with the beliefs of Moses Coady, J.J. Tompkins and of course the St. FX Extension Department, founded to blend education of a practical nature with Catholic philosophy suitable for all levels of society.

MacLellan strove to bring these concepts to reality during his entire term of office with great success. The college was there to give education to youth who could not otherwise afford it. By its second year of existence, practical community-oriented education was launched with night courses in accounting which attracted 80 registrants.[4] The next year a first-year engineering program, with 34 students, was inaugurated. The number of teachers seeking to upgrade their licenses became the bread-and-butter of the college during its first 15 years. By 1953-54 full-time enrolment had risen to 142 students, but part-time students, mainly teachers, numbered 150.[5]

The rapid growth of the college was evidence of both its need and the aptness of its ideals. MacLellan estimated that one-half of the student body would not have been able to attend college or university without XJC.[6] St. FX's summer school classes were even transferred to the Sydney campus, increasing teachers' access to upgrading. Harking back to an earlier community vision, an attempt was made to introduce technology and vocational education to the college since the community still had no such facility. A study was undertaken by a young physics professor, William Reid, to copy programs of Toronto's Ryerson Institute, but the idea was shelved due to the cost of obtaining equipment.[7] An advisory board for the college was established in 1952 in order to study how the college could be of greatest value to the area.[8] Three years later that Board formed the basis of a committee to obtain financial assistance for students, out of which emerged the Xavier Foundation to provide student aid—long before the advent of government loans and bursaries were available.[9]

As courses and enrolment increased, new full-time faculty were hired. In 1955, they included Rev. Everett MacNeil (History), William Reid (Physics), Donald Arseneau (Chemistry), Gerald Aucoin (French), John MacPherson (English), and Rev. Brooks Campbell (Economics and Sociology). Marie O'Keefe and Lois Curry served as registrars, a position that was mainly secretarial and under the firm control of MacLellan. This second group of faculty were all graduates of St. FX, imbued with its ideals and fully supportive of the Junior College's mission. They formed a tight-knit group, many living as neighbours on the newly developed Xavier drive in downtown Sydney.

On May 27, 1952, a small group of men and women slowly made their way down Dorchester Street from the stately Isle Royale Hotel, for decades a cornerstone of Sydney society, to the Lyceum on George Street. It was Cape Breton's first post-secondary academic procession. The question now arose as to the acceptance of these students beyond St. FX. MacLellan was particularly concerned that the transcripts of Xavier Junior College be accepted by Dalhousie, Acadia and Mount Allison, as well. St. FX. President Nicholson insisted that MacLellan confront the presidents of these other universities on his own.

MacLellan did so and received polite receptions and only minor resistance from Acadia and Mount Allison, but he felt Alex Kerr of Dalhousie was lukewarm toward the upstart Junior College. Consequently, when Dalhousie resisted recognition of the Junior College's science courses, MacLellan found the relationship with Dalhousie "embarrassing," and he got little relief from that tension until 1963 when then president of Dalhousie, Henry Hicks, addressing the college's closing exercises, made an official statement of support.[10]

The Department of Education also gave the college headaches, maintaining that its philosophy courses were perhaps too theological. However, teachers who were highly supportive of the college, which was helping to raise their educational and professional standing, brought pressure to bear on the department and the problem was resolved.[11]

Yet there were valid reasons for hesitation to accept the credits of the Junior College. Not only were the facilities relatively primitive, but the library was small and weak. Located on the top storey of the Lyceum, the library shared quarters with classrooms and an assembly area. MacLellan and other priests donated their own book collections and sought contributions from many sources. "Whenever possible," wrote MacLellan, "I begged and borrowed but did not steal."[12] The college's first librarian was Sister Georgina—Marion MacDonald, Congregation of Notre Dame (CND), who began the organization of the collection. She was replaced in 1955 by the now legendary Sister St. Margaret of Scotland—Margaret Beaton, CND. A Gaelic-speaking native of Broad Cove Banks, Inverness County, she was a diminutive bundle of energy and charm who took hold of the library and who literally browbeat the university, the community, and the staff for books. From nothing in 1951, the collection grew to 2,000 by 1962 and to 20,000 by 1965. Each book was lovingly cared for, loaned out wrapped in a plastic bag at that, and only after Sister St. Margaret quizzed the students on their study habits, ancestry and political leanings. Along with MacLellan, Margaret Beaton remains a towering figure of the College's early days and remains in spirit among the collections of the library and the namesake Beaton Institute, to this day.

Rapid growth in staff, students, and library holdings meant space became an almost instant problem. There was very little room for expansion near the Lyceum. Glebe land once owned by the Anglican Diocese of Nova Scotia had been purchased for the erection of St. Anthony Daniel Roman Catholic Church on Alexandra Street in Sydney, and more land was available nearby, but the College could not afford the price. A location outside Sydney was a possibility, but a by-pass to facilitate accessibility was only in the earliest of planning stages at the time. As a result, the area around the Lyceum offered the only hope for immediate expansion. At a time when students didn't have cars, its proximity to bus stops and its downtown Sydney location were convenient. Besides, the St. FX Extension Department, so strongly linked to the College, insisted on the downtown location.

Parcels of land were purchased throughout the fifties and early sixties, beginning with an automobile show yard owned by R.J. Logue, a wealthy entrepreneur and supporter of the college. The land was located diagonally northwest across George Street from the Lyceum.[13] Subsequently, small lots nearby were purchased, while the land directly behind the former Logue property was acquired when the Court House there burnt down in 1961. Although land was slowly being purchased there was no money in hand for the buildings they also needed. The only hope was through private donations. MacLellan had become familiar with the wealthiest Catholics in the area and sought donations from wherever possible, including the William MacDonald family—William, "Billy Senator," as he was known (his father had been a senator), and his two sisters, Mary and Katherine—all of whom were unmarried.

William, a graduate of St. FX, had worked as an accountant and had made a considerable fortune on the stock market. The family was sophisticated, appreciated and collected art and William himself had once given a considerable number of books to Mount St. Vincent. Though

William lacked a relationship with St. FX,[14] it was not long before MacLellan was at his door. The two eventually became good friends. An attempt to gain a land donation from the MacDonalds failed because of legal entanglements, but MacLellan managed to have William divide his estate so that his two sisters and the College received equal shares. The sisters were then persuaded to leave their estate to the College also, resulting in roughly a $400,000 donation from the family,[15] a considerable sum at the time.

And the money certainly was needed. In 1955, the Dominion Bureau of Statistics had forecast an 80 to 90 percent increase in university enrolment by 1965. Previously, one in twenty people of college age attended university; by 1955 the ratio was one in sixteen with a forecast of one in eleven by 1965.[16] In hindsight it is easy to understand the demographics after the end of World War Two, as the first post-war babies neared college age, soon to be followed by the "baby boomers" in ever-increasing numbers.

Added to this increase in potential students, the decline of heavy industrial jobs and the dawn of the age of the knowledge- and technology-based economy called for a more highly educated workforce. More locally, by the late 1950s and early 1960s a prescient fear was being expressed about the future stability of coal and steel in Cape Breton. Ambitious young people and their parents saw that their future, wherever it lay, was not to be in these traditional components of the local economy. University authorities forecast that this attitude would be translated into a need for more scientists and saw enrolment at the college reaching between 250 and 300 by 1965.[17] Faced with the coming deluge of students the St. FX University Board looked at the possibility of restricting registration by raising standards—prudent, but fear was expressed that students would study elsewhere and that the University would face local hostility.[18]

In the mid-1950s there had been some breathing room for the young college. In 1954-55, full-time enrolment at the College reached 154, an increase of only 12 over the previous year; part-time enrolment was 158 of whom 108 were teachers and 52 were studying accounting. By 1956, however, full-time enrolment jumped to 310 and part-time to 226, with the social sciences showing the greatest increase. The College faced an instant space crisis that would never truly be resolved in the first half century of its existence. A number of classes had to be divided into two sections; lab facilities were so filled that a section of the physics lab had to be held at night. Classroom space was leased at nearby Holy Angels High School for Saturday morning classes, now a regular part of the XJC week.[19]

Part-time enrolment also boomed. Between the 1958 and 1959 terms, student population increased by 30 percent, to 310 students. By the latter year, the total College winter term population was 521—that of the whole university just 25 years before.[20] Summer school was also attracting greater numbers, not only locally, but from mainland universities such as Acadia and Dalhousie. In 1959, summer school enrolment was 227, which boosted total College numbers to 700.[21]

For the next few years there was an annual 10 percent increase in the student population. Suddenly, in 1962- 63, for what contemporaries termed "unknown factors," which we know now as the baby boom, enrolment jumped by 20 percent to 1,061, including summer school.[22] In 1964, it totalled 1,315, with 302 full-time students.[23] The alarming rise in numbers even led to thoughts of limiting enrolment to 330 full time students.[24]

THE RELIGIOUS COMPOSITION of the student population was changing as well. As the institution with its Roman Catholic affiliations became more accepted by the community, as much as 30 percent of the enrolment was listed as Protestant or Jewish by 1964.[25] Increased enrolment and student diversity went hand-in-hand with an increase in courses and faculty. Evening courses burgeoned, particularly in part-time enrolment for teachers, accountants, and nurses from St. Rita's School of Nursing.

Courses for full-time students also increased. In 1958, the College was teaching the first two years of arts, the first year of science, college preparatory courses and basic engineering. In 1959, political science was added to the curriculum, and a two-year business administration course was added in 1960. In the same year mechanics and graphics were added to the engineering courses; in 1963 biology was added, followed by night classes in Gaelic in 1964.

Tuition costs were modest at $330 in 1960-61 for full-time students; rising to $385 for Bachelor of Arts, Bachelor of Commerce and Business Administration students, $415 for Bachelor of Science, and $435 for engineering students in 1963-64.[26] These costs were high by local standards, but were needed to cover rising costs of faculty and facilities. One in four students was receiving outside financial aid in the early 1960s, while 20 percent were assisted by the College and five percent by other sources.[27]

Staff numbers of course rose to meet the increased enrolment. In 1960, full-time staff totalled 19, including the registrar, librarian, and her assistant. There were 12 part-time lecturers. These numbers increased to 26 full-time and 13 part-time in 1963-64, with two staff on study leave.[28] This rapid increase in students and staff made expansion of the facilities an absolute necessity. Classes were being held in the Lyceum, in Holy Angels High School and in one of the Navy League Huts, a "homely" single storey building.[29] To make more room, the Extension Department was moved from the Lyceum across George Street to the Standard Brands warehouse, where lunch facilities for male students were also housed.[30]

Conditions in the late 1950s had pressured St. FX to investigate the construction of an arts building. The money received from William MacDonald was being used partly for scholarships, but the remainder, more than $70,000, was available for the new building, and the Canada Council offered $75,000.[31] This could hardly cover costs but, in May 1958, the St. FX Board of Governors agreed to proceed with the construction of an arts building.[32] The University architect, Nils Larson, who represented a North Carolina firm, had already been asked to prepare a plan.[33] In October, plans were ready for a $350,000 building to be located on the site of the Navy League Huts and the adjacent Logue property, which became available late in December, 1958.[34] The Navy League Huts were then demolished, and the building was officially opened July 17, 1960 as the MacDonald Arts Building.[35]

The building was modelled on the colonial Georgian-style buildings found on the Antigonish campus. It contained three levels, the top level being mainly library and staff offices, the second level with five classrooms and two administrative offices and the basement with student services such as a canteen, a small kitchen, a bookstore, a student union office, washrooms, and locker rooms.

The handsome new building had a profound effect on the College campus, giving new life to the institution and witness to its future. As Dr. MacLellan noted at the opening ceremonies, "it is a symbol of the complete support that a worthy cause can expect in this area ... the pledge and a promise of future growth and continuing support."[36] The campus was enlarged further when the College purchased the land formerly occupied by the County Court House.

The cost of the MacDonald building put a serious strain on the finances of the university. It had cost more than $400,000 and, in 1960, the debt on the arts building alone was $182,399. This is enormous considering that the federal grant allocated to the College in 1958-59 was only $44,874 and the provincial grant a negligible $7,520. Student fees amounted to $99,826 that year, while total expenditures were $151,672, which left an operating surplus of $550.[37] Like other institutions of higher learning, financial pressure was increasing.

Though fees rose slowly to help defray expenses, student participation in campus activities also showed a healthy increase. A student union was organized in the first year of the College's operations and, in 1955, the College paper *Junior College Bi-Weekly* was born. Prior to this, XJC news had occupied a page in the St. FX *Xaverian Weekly*. That same year (1955), a drama club was organized by Professor John MacPherson. Other activities, like music appreciation, a glee club, debating society, a

Cercle Française, and a geology club were in operation at the time. Each club had a faculty adviser despite the fact that most faculty taught three full-time and often one part-time course per term. Besides cultural activities, hockey, bowling, football, basketball and even a rifle club were coached by faculty using local high school facilities. Annual winter carnivals and dances rounded out the very active year.

Despite the fact that the College was non-residential and students went home each evening, these activities flourished. Participation was encouraged by faculty and annual X day rallies, whereby students from the parent campus came to Sydney to participate in debates and a banquet. This knit the local college with the larger university, generating a loyalty to and respect for St. FX, where one-third of the graduates of the Junior College eventually studied. Referring to the prevailing atmosphere at St. FX, ultimately transmitted to "little X," Professor John J. Nicholson explained that the "student-teacher relationship was idealized," and that "any fame, status, prestige, or honour conferred on St. FX was due more to its difference from other educational institutions than to its competitive position in academia." He felt the University defined its role differently from its sister universities, due to the important socio-economic role it played in its communities.[38]

During the 1950s, these ideals transmitted by professors, largely graduates of St. FX, kept the Junior College closely linked to the parent campus. The greatest threat to this relationship came first from outside the institution. In the early 1960s, the Province of Nova Scotia began considering making Grade 12 a requirement for university admission. This threatened to make the Junior College a one-year institution which would result in lower enrolment and the loss of its best students. The university organized an enrolment committee to examine this and other problems. Solutions to the impending crisis included offering the second year of science, adding a second year to arts as an honours program, or adding a complete three-year program leading to a BA general degree.[39] Introducing honours in arts would mean Cape Breton students would spend two years on each campus. Others coming from Grade 12 needing remedial work would spend two years in Sydney, but the majority would still spend only one year there.

Seeking an answer to this quandary caused tensions between the campuses. While there was agreement that the "*total* University development" had to be considered, there was no consensus as to what this meant.[40] For example, the Junior College argued for second year courses being added to science in Sydney, along with improved lab facilities, but the main campus representatives felt that this would ultimately mean a decrease in the number of science students in Antigonish.[41] The matter was dropped.

Resentment in Sydney was slowly beginning to mar the relationship with the mainland campus. The Junior College began to feel isolated and very "junior" indeed. College staff were sometimes not invited to departmental meetings in Antigonish.[42] MacLellan was aware of the problem and attempted to have members of the College's Advisory Committee, the forerunner of its Board of Governors, sit on the University Board for "closer liaison" between the institutions, but this was rejected. Instead, it was decided that Board members living in Sydney should attend the Junior College's Advisory Committee meetings.[43] This decision simply isolated Cape Breton from the main campus all the more while the increasing numbers of new staff with no loyalties to St. FX naturally concentrated their efforts on the good of the Junior College and of Cape Breton.

At a meeting of a committee on enrolment and expansion in Antigonish in 1964, MacLellan stressed the need for a permanent joint-university committee to meet at least twice a year to improve relations at both the staff and administrative levels.[44] He reported that there were already calls in Cape Breton that Xavier College be renamed "University of Sydney."[45]

At the same meeting, the XJC representatives again sought more science courses. Dr. William Reid explained that taking second-year science at St. FX was too expensive for Cape Breton students and that consequently, parents were keeping their children from those fields at the very time the need for scientists was growing. He indicated that the lack of contact with upper-level students was preventing students at Sydney from gauging the pace to be followed in the remaining years of their programs. This, he said, led to insecurity on the part of Cape Breton students when attending the Antigonish campus. No decision was reached as to whether a second year in science in Sydney would hurt enrolment in Antigonish.[46] Yet, at a subsequent meeting, the Dean of Science indicated that he was "strongly opposed" to having two institutions competing for faculty members in physics and mathematics.[47] MacLellan secretly fumed at these meetings, and felt the university administration estimated their needs to be more urgent than those of the satellite College, "despite the fact that it was their baby."[48]

The proposed second year in arts at Xavier Junior College was also contentious. A second year was described by St. FX representatives as "inefficient," a move that would "eventually lead to the transfer of the entire faculty to Sydney."[49] This could lead to two universities, which the diocese would never allow.[50] Despite the fears on both sides, relations were generally amicable and there was optimism that some satisfactory arrangements could come about. One hope lay in the possibility of government-sponsored student loans, which was being discussed in the mid-60s. This could allow students from outside the Maritimes to attend XJC, broadening the enrolment base. This was only a vague hope, however, and the Grade 12 entrance requirement remained the single largest threat to the future of the College.[51]

Through all his difficulties in developing the college, MacLellan could always count on the co-operation and support of Bishop John R. MacDonald, who was the ultimate authority in any university dispute. With his death in 1959, a new bishop and chancellor, William E. Power, came on the scene. MacLellan did not feel as comfortable with his new spiritual and university leader. Power was from Montreal and MacLellan thought he neither appreciated the role of the College nor the philosophy of St. FX. He particularly resented the fact that in 1961, Power crippled the College by removing the brilliant Rev. Everett MacNeil, a Canadian History professor, from the College to appoint him his chancellor.[52]

Power had faith in MacLellan, however, offering him the position of Director of the Extension Department, which held no attraction for him. A year later, Power asked him to replace H.J. Somers as President of St. FX itself. At 58, MacLellan felt too old, was worried about his health and did not feel up to facing the problems of university development and the changing attitudes of students in the turbulent mid-60s. He wished the offer had been made earlier, for he had been away from the main campus for 13 years. In the end his conscience, his loyalty to the university and the challenge won out and he accepted.[53]

MacLellan left Sydney July 1, 1964. He had spent his most active years building Xavier College, as it was now officially known, and there can be no doubt that he was the father of the institution he ruled with an iron hand.[54] He brought it literally from nothing to a reputable and indispensable institution. He faithfully tried to transmit the spirit of St. FX to his new campus, and always remained a loyal son of the University. He later wrote that as far as he was concerned, at his departure, "relations with the Alma Mater were first-rate and there was no evidence of the break that would come a decade later."[55] MacLellan was not in concert with members of the staff and community who anxiously sought an independent Bachelor's degree for the College. "That demand," he wrote, "was bound to become increasingly vocal and strong with the passing years. I had tried to make it a first-rate Junior College before moving it to what could be a second-rate Senior College."[56] Whatever its future, Xavier College was providing its community with higher education and the potential for an expanded role in the years to come.

III

College Development, 1965-1974

Fig. 3. Photo by Donald Fewer. Graduates marching into Sacred Heart Church, 1966. Beaton Institute of Cape Breton Studies, University College of Cape Breton. 81-1122-6202.

The early years of the Junior College were characterized by surprising growth, a parental relationship with Saint Francis Xavier University, and deepening relationships within the Industrial Area community. The harmonious interplay of these three elements, whereby the growing College sent its graduates to St. FX helping ensure a stable enrolment there, while enabling the latter to carry out its mission of community education and development in the Industrial Area, benefited all parties concerned.

During its second decade however, this balance was upset. The Industrial Area began to undergo serious economic problems in the mid-sixties which it hoped the College could help resolve with practical educational strategies. The College's desire to meet these needs and to maintain its population base, for steady enrolment, spurred it to enhance its programs. In doing so it came into conflict with the parent campus which was worried about losing or dividing its programs and students with the College, threatening the viability of both. In turn, people in the Industrial Area supported the College's bid for higher degrees so that the two became allies against any off-island body, whether governmental or educational, which threatened their growing symbiotic relationship.

The effort to satisfy these concerns, which would result in the establishment of the College of Cape Breton, took the better part of a decade. The meeting of the challenge resulted initially in the enlargement and finally the building of a new campus, the result of an amalgamation of the College with the Nova Scotia Eastern Institute of Technology (NSEIT) into a new and innovative institution with a range of educational opportunities inconceivable only a few years before.

Rev. Donald Francis Campbell took up his duties as Principal of Xavier Junior College June 30, 1964. A native of Sydney, like many talented young Cape Bretoners, he had completed his Bachelor's degree at St. FX in 1945.[1] He was ordained to the priesthood in 1949, and went on to postgraduate work at the University of London, receiving his PhD in education at the Catholic University of America in Washington, DC, in

1956. Immediately afterward he was appointed head of the Education Department at St. FX, then Dean of Arts.

Campbell's appointment to XJC was a vote of confidence in his proven cool perception of facts and his talent for consensus building. He was expected to represent the interests of his alma mater in the industrial area and to further its role in the overall development of Eastern Nova Scotia. At the same time, it was expected that a native of Sydney would understand the aspirations of the College and of the whole Industrial Area.

Campbell's management style was different from MacLellan's. His attitudes were more collegial and he was less likely to micromanage than his predecessor. Father "Charlie Beag" MacDonald, the Director of Continuing Education, became his mentor, his informal, candid manner complementing Campbell's reserved, diplomatic approach to management.[2] At the time of his appointment, the College was growing and expansion was in the air. At the same time the challenge of the Grade 12 entrance requirement for admission to the arts degree was threatening to cut enrolment and endanger the very existence of the institution. The attempt to meet this challenge strained relations with the parent institution during the first decade of Campbell's leadership.

In the meantime, enrolment at the Sydney campus continued to increase. In 1964, there were 381 full-time students at Xavier. This increased to 696 in 1970-71, but declined to 537 in 1973-74. Part-time enrolment, however, which stood at 392 in 1964-65, grew to 832 in 1974. Even more spectacular was the growth of part-time non-credit courses in adult education which spiralled from 63 in 1964-65 to 1,197 ten years later. When these figures were added to the number of students in summer school and intersession courses, figures topped 3,100 students in 1973-74. Enrolment reflected the changing demographics and economy of the Industrial Area of Cape Breton during that period which in turn affected how the College met the challenges they represented.[3]

Once again increased enrolment called for more space. When Malcolm MacLellan left in 1964, plans were already underway for a much-needed science building to replace the inadequate facilities in the Lyceum. In April of that year, a St. FX university committee of enrolment and expansion had suggested that, with current facilities, enrolment at XJC should be held at 330 full-time students. If a new library and science building could be built, the committee felt the college could accommodate 550.[4]

The year previously, MacLellan had appointed a joint committee of the faculty and the College's non-denominational Advisory Board to study ways of obtaining the funds for a new science building. At the same time, options were being obtained on adjacent properties.[5] When 50 more students than expected enrolled in 1964, the situation became more urgent. Consequently, on October 19, 1964, the "Science For Xavier" $500,000 campaign for building and equipment, had been launched with M.R. Campbell, Works Manager at Dominion Coal and Steel Company, as chairman and Principal MacLellan as honourary chairman. This was the College's first general call for community assistance.[6]

Appeals were made particularly to local businesses and industry on the grounds that there was a direct relationship between the industrial future of Cape Breton and the availability of personnel with a science education.[7] However, credit unions, labour unions and teachers' organizations also contributed.[8] As well, the College was the first institution in Nova Scotia to take advantage of the newly inaugurated provincial grants for capital construction.[9] Within less than a month $209,000 was pledged and plans for another building in the style of the MacDonald Arts Building were underway. Structures on adjacent properties on George Street were demolished and, on August 12, 1965, a contract was let for the construction of the building which was completed early in 1966 at a total cost of $700,000, occupied that September and officially opened on December 3 by the University Chancellor, Bishop William E. Power.[10]

The community's direct contribution to the erection of the science building strengthened its sense of ownership of Xavier College. During the campaign the community had been made to realize that almost two million dollars had been invested locally by the institution and that the College would "keep our sons and daughters and education dollars at home."[11]

Fig. 4. Photo by Owen Fitzgerald. George Street arts and science buildings of Xavier Junior College, 1960s. Courtesy Robert Morgan.

The science building, like the arts building, was a three-storey structure in the colonial Georgian style. The basement housed physics laboratories, two classrooms and locker space convertible to a future computer centre or research lab. The first floor displayed in its foyer, a modernistic bas-relief by Rev. Thomas Roach of St. FX—the College's first commissioned work of art. Nearby was the administrative area, which could be converted into labs, the faculty offices, a physics and a biology lab and a large 93 square metres (1,000 square feet) classroom. The top floor contained two more classrooms, chemistry labs, a drafting lab for engineering students and a dark room.

Anticipating that even this space would not be enough the College purchased a private residence, MacLeod House, on adjacent Nepean Street in 1965. Part of the building was used as a study hall to alleviate the overcrowded library in the arts building. The second floor provided space for three faculty offices. The top floor became the home of the Student Union, the College newspaper *Excalibur*, and the yearbook offices. The space they vacated in the arts building was occupied by the college book store. The drama club was in the dusty basement. Decoration of the

MacLeod House, which soon became a College landmark, was undertaken by the students who used the building as a gathering place and campus centre.[12]

Space was still inadequate. As early as 1955-56, an internal college study had found that the high cost of properties in downtown Sydney would prevent expansion there.[13] In October, 1966, the College's Advisory Board and the executive of the University Board of Governors decided to hire the firm of Taylor, Leiberfeld and Heldman to suggest solutions.[14] Five months later, "Leiberfeld 1," as the report was known, concluded that the land in the vicinity of the College was inadequate for an academic body that might expand to as much as one or two thousand students if degrees were ever offered. Parking would be at a minimum and the expense of buying properties would rise to between 3 and 4.7 million dollars on the unlikely condition that owners would sell at assessed prices.[15] Other properties examined, such as the Rifle Range, Cossitt's Lake and Rotary Park areas in the city's outskirts were found to be even more expensive, as well as difficult to access.

Leiberfeld favoured the acquisition of the Department of National Defence property at Victoria Park at the extreme north end of the Sydney peninsula. The 7-hectare (17.8 acre) site, located 300 metres or a six-minute walk from the campus, could accommodate college buildings for up to 2,000 students, but not parking space for everyone. The report indicated that transference of title to the College would be relatively inexpensive, with total outlay for land and new buildings at between 2.8 million dollars for a 1,000-student campus to 5.03 million dollars for a 2,000-student degree-granting College.[16] They praised the Park's commanding position over the harbour, dismissed the presence of a nearby cement plant and oil tanks and claimed that "the presence of the Dosco steel mill to the east of Victoria Park does not appear to be too detrimental, particularly as the prevailing winds blow the exhaust from the furnaces away from the Park."[17]

The Board of Governors appointed a committee to examine the recommendations and report by October. Faculty on the whole was lukewarm to Victoria Park, for environmental and aesthetic concerns, as well as the fragmentation of the campus. They were more concerned with the need for expanded offerings and wanted a further study made of the feasibility of a four-year degree program for the college.[18] These opinions reflected a heated public controversy that broke out while the Leiberfeld study was underway. During the summer of 1966, Sydney's Kiwanis Club approved a motion calling for full university status for the College. This found support from the Sydney Board of Trade, the Sydney Steel Union and the *Cape Breton Post* which openly advocated a four-year degree-granting institution within the city with "no more beating around the bush."[19]

Tensions grew. A radical student paper at St. FX, probably with tongue in cheek, claimed that XJC was too locally oriented, that it encouraged quirks of "Caper speech," that academic standards were lower there and that the college simply weakened the parent institution academically and should be closed.[20] These allegations hit a sore point and caused a backlash that eventually resulted in the editor's resignation.[21]

But the damage had been done and the degree controversy was now out in the open. Malcolm MacLellan, now president of St. FX, tried to cool tempers by commenting that two-year Colleges had a "special role" and that government could not be expected to duplicate educational services. He reiterated his deeply held feelings that to have a first-rate university "seems wiser than to end up with two or even more second-rate and inferior institutions."[22]

In the midst of all the controversy, the College continued to move forward with new courses. The second year of science was introduced in 1966 and the Business Administration program, previously available on a part-time basis, received its first full-time appointments.[23] Third- and fourth-year courses were added in part-time programs, bringing senior courses to the College for the first time. Rev. C.W. MacDonald inaugurated a credit-free program in 1965, which opened the College to the community more than ever. People with no academic background could attend ten-week courses without having to complete exams or assignments. Despite some academic suspicion of the program, many of these people eventually made their way into degree programs. Courses such as communication, science, man and the modern world, psychology, history, industrial personnel relations, and Bible studies opened doors to people who may never have been exposed to higher learning. Fifty-two people enrolled in 1965; 351 in 1967; 417 in 1968.[24]

With the growing interest in new courses, by the time Leiberfeld reported in October, 1967, students, faculty and the community were as interested in obtaining degree courses in Sydney as in the location of the College. So when he received the Leiberfeld Report, MacLellan, whatever his private feelings, appointed the firm to undertake a second study on the possibilities of a degree-granting institution in Sydney.

On October 13, a dramatic announcement threatened the expansion. Plans were announced to close the Steel Plant, throwing 3,200 people out of work, and the community became involved in a whirlwind of speeches, marches and speculation. What would now become of Xavier College? "There is no doubt about it," Principal Campbell asserted, "if this [the steel plant closure] happened our enrolment of about 400 full-time and 520 part-time students would be cut drastically next year." He added that "any drop out, would force us to consider our future here in Sydney and indeed future plans for St. FX under which we operate." Yet government assistance for the Cape Breton economy would mean the College would be needed more than ever.[25] A few days later, after encouraging signs from politicians, Campbell announced that plans to expand Xavier would continue.[26]

It was in this atmosphere of economic uncertainty that Taylor, Leiberfeld and Heldman prepared their second report investigating the growth and development patterns of St. FX and how Little X could provide better educational opportunities for its beleaguered community. To the Cape Breton public the question boiled down to degree-granting status and physical expansion of the college. Leiberfeld forecast deterioration in the economic conditions in Eastern Nova Scotia, resulting in a shrinkage of the population base at a time when the percentage of students from the local area was a growing percentage of enrolment. It also predicted that the university participation rate would lag behind the rest of Canada, resulting in a decline in enrolment after 1980.[27]

The report assumed different models for the relationship between the two campuses. If the current structure remained, the University, including the Sydney branch, could expect operating surpluses until 1985-86. This model, however, would not meet the Sydney metropolitan area's aspirations for equality of educational opportunity. On the other hand, an integrated two-campus university with XJC operating degree programs in specified areas, would mean a surplus in the operating budgets until 1985-86, when a small deficit could be expected. This model forecast the Antigonish enrolment stabilizing at 2,400, with the Sydney campus serving as a feeder to help maintain that level. By keeping the structure of the parent University flexible, moving the business degree, for example, and other courses as needed to Sydney, predicted Sydney enrolment decline could be minimized. As well, at least a few degree programs could be offered there to satisfy the aspirations of the Cape Breton public.

As far as full parallel development for the Sydney campus offering the same degrees and courses as Antigonish, however, the consultants felt it was "financially impractical ...[and] would fail to permit the University to take advantage of the potential for academic quality that enrolment expansion can make possible."[28] The "flexible integrated structure" recommended by the report would see arts majors dropped in Sydney, with business administration retained until 1984, when it predicted overall enrolment would decline. Sydney would have to bear the brunt of this decline since Antigonish had residences to maintain and a much higher capital investment.

The report went on to elaborate ways in which communications could be improved between the two campuses so that courses need not be duplicated. Use of the telephone, "tele-lectures" or television could be used to save money. Library books could be shuttled between the campuses by special buses.[29]

The following November, the University Council appointed a committee of six, three from each campus, to study and make recommendations on the report. After five meetings the committee was unable to reach a consensus and each made a separate report.[30] The Antigonish members favoured a new Sydney campus with new classrooms, offices, library, and student services centre and possibly a gymnasium, but otherwise it should continue to offer its existing programs. They noted "the drain-off of major and honors students, which would undoubtedly result from the extension of Xavier College programs to the Junior or Junior and Senior levels, could only result in a decrease in the viability of major and honors programs and in the capacity of the University to attract superior scholars."[31] The trio also found that the aspirations of the Antigonish community, which was economically dependent on St. FX, were as justifiable as industrial Cape Breton's call for a university. A weakened university with lower standards and prestige would help no one.[32]

The representatives from Xavier College indicated that they "emphatically" did not support the establishment of a separate degree-granting institution in Sydney. While not supporting the business degree for Sydney alone, they were largely supportive of Leiberfeld, calling for more flexible and integrated programs between the campuses, using contemporary developments in inter-campus communication. They claimed this would allow the development of the four-year general Arts degree in Sydney, to the benefit of the whole university, including adults. It would raise the educational level of the area and improve economic opportunity, attracting "a better qualified, more stable and contented faculty."[33] The attitudes of the two sides showed little change over the next five years.

The University Council met in April 1970 and approved the junior and senior years of a general BA at Xavier College, by a narrow margin of eleven to eight.[34] This recommendation was approved by the University faculty by the wide margin of 83 to 47 at its April 23 meeting.[35] These actions received the support of the Industrial Cape Breton community, of course. The Mature Students Association also backed the call for a third year to help married former employees of DEVCO, who found going to St. FX too expensive and a mere "concession to tradition."[36] The plan still lacked the approval of the Board.

Meanwhile, Leiberfeld's site recommendations were under scrutiny. The report's approval of Victoria Park had found little favour. Faculty in 1968 had rejected it on aesthetic and accessibility grounds and called for a site near a new Sydney highway bypass.[37] By then it was already clear that the Victoria Park site was unattainable. Despite assistance from politicians and DEVCO the Department of National Defence refused to sell the property for less than $1.5 million, though it was assessed at about $273,000, and confirmed its "continuing requirements for this site" in October 1968.[38]

Any fears as to the future of Industrial Cape Breton and Xavier College were laid to rest in October of 1968, however, when Premier G.I. Smith, delighted with the profits of the provincially owned steel mill, pledged a $50 million expansion there.[39] This announcement counteracted the arguments of some St. FX faculty opposed to expansion in Sydney on the grounds of the economic instability of the area. As a result, the Board Of Governors approved motions for the acquisition of land near the Sydney bypass and for the planning of new buildings.[40] Campbell had already met with Arthur Murphy, chairman of the province's University Grants Committee, who suggested that the College make its plans and the Committee would consider the costs.[41]

The College therefore began to assemble 44 acres of land on the shores of Cossitt Lake near the juncture of the Sydney bypass and the Glace Bay highway. In September, Cape Breton County Council approved the sale of the land valued at $15,500. The College covered the complete cost using money from the MacDonald estate.[42] The total cost for the new campus was estimated at seven million dollars, which was submitted for approval to the University Grants Committee in mid-April.[43] Within a month the committee approved in principle the relocation and hopes were high that work would soon begin.[44] The Toronto firm of F.W. Woodcock was commissioned to draw up plans for site development the following spring.[45]

During the summer of 1970, however, things began to unravel. In June, Murphy informed Nova Scotia university presidents that the Grants Committee was examining the Grade 12 requirements for admission to university in the light of possible new colleges in South West Nova Scotia and the Agricultural College in Truro. He suggested that the committee was recommending to the Minister of Education that the decision on the Grade 12 requirement be postponed until matters were clarified in relation to these institutions.[46] This caused the St. FX representatives on the board to explain that they felt the only reason the University Council and faculty had approved the junior and senior years at Xavier College was because they had expected the requirement to be in place by 1972. This was now uncertain, and they felt the whole issue of the BA should be re-examined by a special committee of the board, called the Xavier Expansion Committee, while the expansion went ahead as approved by the University Grants Committee. A motion to this effect was passed by a majority of one vote, and revealed a deep split between the two campuses.[47]

The reaction in Sydney was predictable. The *Cape Breton Post* called the BA delay a "red herring," attempting to hinder the educational development of Cape Breton.[48] The Xavier Expansion Committee, with D.F. Campbell and M.R. Campbell representing the College, met during the summer and appointed two firms of consultants: Kates, Peat, Marwick and Company, to study enrolment projections for academic programs; and Touche Ross to assess costs of development in Cape Breton. In late October, the committee reported with various models of academic development.[49] Against a background of unrest in Sydney, the Board Of Governors, by a margin of only two votes, ignored the consultants' reports and agreed with the recommendation that the general BA be offered in Sydney.[50]

This time, the reaction in Sydney was ecstatic and the next day students staged a downtown parade in celebration.[51] The whole issue of the BA had now become more emotional than ever and the cause of Cape Breton's development and Island pride was now involved. The usual December celebration of "X-day" affirming the links between the campuses was called "absurd" and "boring," a mere tribute to the "gaping yawn of tradition."[52] An economics professor from St. FX, William Woodfine, a strong opponent of the degree program at Xavier College, warned that any inclusion of a degree program in an application for expansion to the University Grants Committee could lead to the rejection of both the expansion and the BA plans entirely. In response, it was pointed out that the seven-million-dollar expansion had already been approved by the committee—though privately, D.F. Campbell had misgivings that Woodfine might be correct.[53] Uncertainty led the College to suspend Woodcock's investigation of possible college structures.[54]

The fears proved well-founded. In the fall of 1970, the Conservative government of G.I. Smith was replaced by the Liberals under Gerald Regan. The new government placed a moratorium on capital expenditures, including university expenditures. Early in the new year word was received that the Grants Committee had recommended against the request for a four-year program at Xavier College on the grounds that "they felt the Province had sufficient degree-granting institutions." Shortly after, they added that even the relocation project should be denied since the new government had placed a moratorium on capital expenditures.[55] The Industrial Area was shocked at this new turn of events, which neatly threw the whole problem into the lap of the government.

Premier Regan was caught in a vice between the Grants Committee and the educational demands of the Sydney area electorate. He agreed to go to Sydney February 3 to announce the start on the modernization of Sydney Steel. Students demanded that he meet with them and the public as well, and that afternoon at the Sydney Forum amidst the boos of 2,000 students as well as the public and local officials, Regan spoke. He claimed that he had just recently become aware of the Xavier question, disclaimed having appointed the current Grants Committee, said it would be dangerous to overrule them and suggested that the question be referred back to them. The audience became agitated and Regan then added that "if they are unable to resolve the question, we're prepared to consider whether Government will have to intervene and find some way to make some decision."[56] He finished by saying, "we are absolutely committed to the continuance of a Community College here in Sydney. We are absolutely committed that there shall be an expansion of [the] Campus....[57]

The tired premier gave the same basic speech that evening at the Steel Workers' Hall, but in a more rambling and vague manner.[58] He met with community leaders that evening who tried to pressure him to control the Grants Committee. Reaction to the premier's statements was mixed. D.F. Campbell was "rather happy" with them, but C.W. MacDonald was "more bullish." About the premier he said: "His problem is, and we appreciate it, how to save face with the factions opposing the program. He will have to ask his conscience which comes first, the legitimate rights of a community for a degree college or saving face with certain factions."[59] MacDonald was pointing at other universities who were clamoring for more money and who he saw as pressuring the government and the Grants Committee to hold back the growth in Sydney on the grounds that there were already enough centres of higher learning in Nova Scotia.

Matters remained at a stalemate during the late winter and early spring of 1971, the government sending mixed messages sympathetic to the College's relocation without budgeting for such a move, while Regan's Education Minister, Peter Nicholson, professed admiration for Inverness MLA Jim MacLean's courage in opposing the BA at Xavier College. Indeed, the plan for relocation had become fused with the BA proposal to the detriment of both.[60] Behind the scenes, the University and the Grants Committee sparred over the cost of the relocation until the end of March, when the Committee informed the university they would discuss relocation with the full cabinet after the legislature prorogued later in the spring. Meanwhile, they refused to reverse their recommendation on the BA degree.[61]

Faced with government inaction, university representatives decided to simplify matters by seeking expansion only, dropping the seemingly futile BA campaign.[62] Desperate for immediate space, Campbell received board permission to locate eight new classrooms and 20 offices in mobile units at the rear of the college, the money to be taken from the MacDonald estate.[63] The "Portable Classrooms," as they were called (though they never moved), were ready by September, but did little to enhance the appearance of the campus which to many seemed "degrading in comparison to the affluent appearance of the Antigonish campus."[64]

As the provincial government pondered the direction to follow with the college, the federal government, in the form of the Cape Breton Development Corporation (DEVCO) stepped in. DEVCO had been established in 1968 to see to the orderly closure of the local coal mines and to replace the jobs thus lost with new industrial development. Realizing that St. FX did not have the required equity of ten percent (1 to 1.5 million dollars) toward the construction of a new Sydney campus St. FX President MacLellan and Campbell, with the active support of B. Alistair Graham, Executive Secretary and Vice President of DEVCO, began discussions with DEVCO officials. DEVCO realized that the higher education of the local population was an essential component of any economic expansion. In 1971, Tom Kent, an Ottawa economist and bureaucrat, whose wife was an academic, was appointed president of DEVCO and, by October of 1971, Kent and College officials came to an agreement. A $500,000 matching grant, as well as a $500,000 loan, would move the College, probably to Cossitt Lake, with the stipulation that money be repaid through the sale of the College's downtown buildings.[65] These offers were kept secret by all parties pending new developments.

One of those developments came in November from the provincial government: the decision to study a possible union between Xavier College and the Nova Scotia Eastern Institute of Technology (NSEIT). This revived the practical ideal of blending technology and liberal arts in a Cape Breton college, in which both MacLellan and Campbell had shown an interest. In November 1968, the NSEIT had been opened with 80 students, in order, according to John E. Terry, its first principal, "to prepare Cape Breton's young men and women to meet the challenge of tomorrow's technological world."[66] Technologies offered were mineral, mechanical engineering, civil engineering, chemical, electrical and electronic engineering. "Eastern Tech" was located on the Grand Lake Road, between Sydney and Glace Bay with a capacity for 899 students. The facilities, costing $3 million to build and having $2 million in equipment, were opulent in comparison with Xavier's. Courses like business and engineering technology were geared to the so-called new economy and though original enrolment was low (less than 100 in 1968) the potential for growth was great and staff morale was high. They felt they were fulfilling a vital role in Cape Breton's educational structure.[67]

Campbell, hoping for some form of union, had been disappointed when the NSEIT was located so far from the Xavier campus. Back in late 1969 he and MacLellan had been called to a meeting in Port Hawkesbury by Gerald Doucet, Minister of Education in the Tory government of G.I. Smith, to discuss the possible relocation of Xavier to the Cossitt Lake site. The Minister told them that it would be a better idea to join with NSEIT than to pursue the BA. Campbell objected that he was committed to it, "and if we could offer degrees in some sort of sharing with NSEIT, then I would see my way clear to actively promote the idea [of amalgamation]."[68]

As luck would have it, within a year there was a change in government, but the new Minister of Education, Peter Nicholson, wasted no time approaching Campbell, Terry and a number of their colleagues, and between 1970 and 1972, they met for a series of discussions concerning the proposed merger. They broke into subgroups studying all aspects of a merger, such as admissions, pre-engineering and science, sharing facilities, credit transfers and extension as well as possible models in Canada and the United States. After some discussion, a plan to include the nearby Canadian Coast Guard College in the plan was shelved, as its federal mandate would simply complicate an already difficult challenge.[69]

By the fall of 1971, while relocation of the College and a union with NSEIT were being considered, another old topic came up for debate: that of the relationship between the college and St. FX proper. The mutual aggravation between the two campuses had not abated and there was growing realization that "unless some solution was found to the 'problem' and unless considerably more ingenuity is displayed than has been the case to date, the University might very well be in serious trouble."[70]

The need to prepare new bylaws for the University precipitated the need for a study of the interrelationship, and a committee was appointed by the University Senate, which reported in April 1972.[71]

The committee held open hearings on both campuses. The results in Antigonish were disappointing, "probably reflecting the ignorance of the problem, apathy, weariness or a combination of both."[72] In Sydney there was "anger, resentment and bitterness."[73] The old problems of location, course allocations and degree-granting remained. Yet the committee realized that at least some changes must occur at the Sydney campus. It recommended that the name "Xavier College" be changed to "St. Francis Xavier University Sydney Campus," in an attempt to foster the dual campus concept. They added that the BA and BBA should be offered in Sydney by 1975 with the residence requirement waived. In recognition of what was already underway the committee recommended that program cooperation take place between XJC, NSEIT and the Canadian Coast Guard College, and that research links be forged with the staff at the Fortress of Louisbourg. Changes in the relationship between the Sydney and Antigonish campuses, such as greater budget coordination, library cooperation and the implementation of the senior year BA program at Sydney for mature students by September 1972, would be dealt with in the upcoming modification of the university bylaws.[74]

The Senate, however, failed to agree to the plan for offering the BA degree at Sydney and, after a five-hour session, voted by a wide margin to postpone further discussions on the topic until October, 1974.[75] Other advances at Sydney, such as the appointment of departmental chairs and the name change to "St. Francis Xavier University, Sydney Campus," were allowed.[76]

These concessions just weren't enough. The decision to shelve the BA yet again roused the Cape Breton campus, and a general assembly was called which recommended a "split from the main university and a ... Cape Breton university which would be a new type of university ... adapted to the needs of people," such as housing, pollution, welfare, and the development of local Cape Breton culture in such things as music and the other arts.[77]

Campbell, with characteristic insight, envisaged the possible fulfillment of an old aspiration: "If we are imaginative and resourceful enough we can pioneer a totally new concept in university education here."[78] To cool tempers, he promised part-time courses for the third- and fourth-year students and to rent more space in the recently occupied Logue Building in downtown Sydney, a few blocks south of the rest of the campus.[79] As well, the University Senate decided to investigate the overall organization of the university. They appointed a Committee on Structures in May with three representatives from each campus.[80] It met eleven times between June 29, 1972, and February 15, 1973. The committee was charged with working out the plans for a multi-campus university. It discussed the idea of each campus having its own principal and similar officials for local needs, all of whom would fall under an overall administration with its president and senior officials in charge of the needs of the university as a whole. It soon became clear that this arrangement would alienate the Antigonish campus, and would be unworkable, particularly since the provincial government was leaning toward some sort of separate organization for the Sydney operation that would involve the NSEIT.

The committee consulted Dr. T.B.H. Symons, former president of Trent University, who spurred them on in their final decision, which was "to proceed, with deliberate and reasonable haste, in the direction of establishing an independent institution in Sydney." Such an institution could offer innovative degrees tailored to the needs of Cape Breton and would be in a stronger position to exert an "academic and humanistic influence" on the proposed new institution combining NSEIT, Xavier College and possibly the Coast Guard College. The new institution would be affiliated with St. FX and offer its programs with the approval of the University Senate.[81] The committee thereupon called for a timetable to be worked out towards the eventual independence of the Sydney operation.

All the while the university was debating the future of the Sydney campus, signs of the government's desire to speed the unification process had become apparent. A month before the senate subcommittee's report, Premier Gerald Regan, following discussions with Campbell and John Terry on the union of Xavier College and NSEIT, decided to appoint a Committee on Post-Secondary Education in Cape Breton.[82] Its report would seal the fate of the Sydney campus, its location and eventually the offering of the BA. The group met for a year and reported January 31, 1973. It was composed of representatives from both campuses of the university, DEVCO, the provincial government and the University Grants Committee.[83] All the pressures from other wary universities, conflicting disciplines, the parent campus, and the local community came together in the Committee which called upon the expertise of Joseph Lauwerys, Director of the Atlantic Institute of Education to suggest some models for its guidance.

Lauwerys' report envisaged a new kind of institution in Sydney, "a unique venture in higher education," which "is innovative in that it would have its technical and academic components as equal partners."[84] He added that "it would have a strong academic component from Xavier and an equally strong technical component from NSEIT."[85] It would not be a polytechnic college since its academic wing would not be subordinate to its technical one. Instead, it would unite the humanities and technology in new ways, not only through courses and research, but in areas such as technology assessment and transfer.[86] It would extend the imaginative ways that Xavier had already shown in working for and with the community for its development through institutes and continuing education.[87] Such an institution would attract scholars and students to build the critical mass needed to achieve these goals.

The bulk of Lauwerys' report was taken up with the mechanics for the establishment of the new institution and its location. Lauwerys suggested that an administrative council composed of representatives of government, the university, DEVCO, student and community representatives be appointed to organize the institution within five years by integrating the academic and technical wings of the institution in a way that would lead to Bachelor of Technology degrees as well as the Bachelor of Arts, or Bachelor of Commerce.[88] The new campus would have its own funding, which would effectively separate it from the parent University. Lauwerys had Frank Woodcock and Associates, an Ontario-based project management firm, analyze costs of various locations for the institution.[89] Woodcock found that there was no compelling financial reason for choosing any one of the Cossitt Lake, Victoria Park or the NSEIT site, but he favoured Cossitt Lake or Victoria Park.[90] His main concern was that the decision be made quickly, and that a specific schedule be set up dealing with location, building construction and integration of the two institutions.

Most of Lauwerys' recommendations found favour with the guiding personality behind the Committee's work, the new Minister of Education, Allan Sullivan, a Cape Bretoner who was actively committed to the birth of the new institution. He favoured a union of the XJC and NSEIT campuses at the latter's location and the acquisition of the BA. With the rest of the committee, he endorsed the plan for an innovative institution to be known as a college, with an administrative council eventually to become an independent board of governors with representation from St. FX to manage the transition and operation of the college. The institution was to offer the general BA through St. FX by the fall of 1975. By July, 1974, the board was to have its own budget received directly from government for all programs with an initial grant of $100,000 to cover organizational costs during 1973. Sullivan's strong hand is apparent in the committee's recommendation to locate the college on the property owned by the provincial government at the site of the NSEIT on the Sydney-Glace Bay highway.[91]

The report swept away further objections as to the status and location of the new institution. On February 16, 1973, the University Senate and faculty approved the first draft of the report. The next day the Sydney faculty assented to it on the condition that its academic concerns regarding course offerings and the BA be recognized.[92]

The report was brought before the St. FX Board Of Governors on 18 February. They realized that objections were useless. If the NSEIT site, for example, was not approved, the moratorium on capital building would not be lifted and there would be no new campus. They knew it was "apparent the university [had] no alternative but to accept the government's proposal."[93] The college would be located in what Lauwerys called "splendid isolation" on free government-owned land.[94] Everyone agreed that the academic quality of the institution must be carefully guarded lest the institution "degenerate to a technical institute."[95] Finally the board agreed to accept its senate subcommittee's recommendation that "this new entity" maintain an affiliation with St. FX while entering into negotiations with officials of the government and NSEIT for the relocation of the campus and the safeguard of Xavier's academic status, its staff and students.[96]

Meanwhile, in order to strengthen the academic aspect as well as enrolment of the present college, Campbell and Reid argued before the Senate that the junior year and BA be offered at Xavier in the fall of 1973. The final year would ensure that Xavier would not become a one-year institution. The St. FX component, however, more concerned with loss of students to Sydney at a time of declining enrolments and a growing deficit, rejected this plea.[97] Mature students, on the other hand, were to be allowed to work toward their BA at Xavier.

This decision resulted in an explosion of wrath in Sydney. Students staged a demonstration culminating in the burning in effigy the parent University's Antigonish administration building.[98] The usually cool Donald Campbell stated that the Senate's action showed that St. FX, though unable to solve the problems of higher education in Cape Breton, was yet unwilling to approve expansion programs needed there. He called for government officials to step in to ensure the viability of the Sydney operation. The alternatives were affiliation with another university or a campaign for a separate university charter for the new institution.[99]

Campbell was under considerable stress at the time. His chief mentor, Father Charles MacDonald, had been killed in an avalanche at a ski resort in Innsbruck, Austria at the end of March, and these added rejections were almost too much to bear.[100] The outpouring of emotion at "Father Charlie's" death and the community's agitation over the rejection of the junior year and the degree, brought feelings to a peak. Community leaders urged Campbell to stand firm for a university charter for the new institution.[101] The Junior College faculty joined in the chorus, blaming the Antigonish operation's unwillingness to make capital expenditures at XJC for fear of reducing the profit from their "branch plant" in Sydney.[102]

In the midst of this pressure Sullivan, Campbell, and St. FX President Malcolm MacDonnell with the strong support of DEVCO, managed to obtain government approval of the Special Committee's recommendations for the merger of Xavier College and NSEIT by May 10, 1973.[103] In effect, Cabinet had approved Canada's first "humanitechnical" college, the first "effective integration of the degree-granting humanities and technical programs in Canada."[104] This innovative institution, in affiliation with St. FX, would qualify students for academic and technological degrees and diplomas. A self-governing Board would not be under the jurisdiction of either the Department of Education or the Board of St. FX, but would operate on its own as of July 1, 1974. The goal was to gain the BA by 1975, while working out new programs. This would not be easy since the College was warned that it must avoid competition with other universities who, like St. FX, were beginning to feel the pinch of rising costs and declining enrolment.[105] This stipulation would serve as a burden, but also as a stimulant for the new institution's development for years to come.

D.F. Campbell, as interim president, began working with John Terry, NSEIT president, during the summer of 1973 in order to find ways to develop the project. Meanwhile, meetings of the College's General Assembly, which had been organized two years previously by the late Rev. Charles MacDonald to keep the community up to date on developments, were held.[106]

By the fall, Campbell had appointed two important working committees composed of representatives of both institutions, one to design a unique BA degree, and a Program Planning Committee to examine new programs for the new entity.[107] Besides this, a 31-member Advisory Committee or Board for Post-Secondary Education in Cape Breton was also appointed. It was composed of students, faculty and administration of both campuses, as well as mainland and government representatives, whose job was to advise the Minister of Education on the planning and organization of the college.[108] They approved the association of the NSEIT and St. FX Sydney campus. This body would eventually become the Board Of Governors of the new college.

It seemed that, almost fortuitously, the earlier hopes for an innovative institution of higher learning dedicated to all facets of learning and firmly rooted in its community, was about to be realized. The challenge was now to make this entity operational by charting a course untravelled by any other institution of higher learning in Canadian history.

IV

The College of Cape Breton, 1974-1983

With the approval of the union of Xavier and NSEIT in principle the practical work of operating the new entity and preparing for an act of incorporation had to begin. The College authorities, headed by Donald Campbell and John Terry, spent the summer of 1973 drawing up budgets for the respective faculties for presentation to government. It was a strange time. The new institution had no name, Xavier was still operating in St. FX property, but it was drawing up its own budget.[1] The Advisory Board, not yet a Board Of Governors, held its first meeting in November focusing on plans for incorporation.[2]

Although classes began in September, seemingly as usual, students at NSEIT understandably felt left out of the picture. As an executive member of their Students' Association put it, "Xavier needs us but we don't need nor do we care if we ever see Xavier;" nor did he relish having the Institute's new facilities being taken over by the "Little 'X' buzzards."[3]

Fig. 5. Photo by Donald Fewer. Portable classrooms deal with overcrowding at George Street campus, c1975. Beaton Institute of Cape Breton Studies, University College of Cape Breton. 81-1137-6217.

Despite such feelings, there was no student unrest as work on the incorporation rolled into the fall and winter.

NSEIT faculty also felt a certain distrust for the new institution. Amalgamation plans had progressed with little input from them. Indeed, at a meeting of Nova Scotia Technology Institute directors in Halifax, John Terry learned that the merger plans had already been finalized. Staff back home refused to believe this account of events, believing instead that he had gone there to avoid facing them himself. Such lack of communication could only sow the seeds of suspicion among the technology faculty, making the union of the two institutions more difficult.[4] The technologists complained that they were under pressure to acquiesce to what they saw as a "shotgun marriage," in which the academics would hold the upper hand. How would the world of "doers" get along with the world of "thinkers?" How could a group used to line-authority reporting fare with the rough-and-tumble world of collegiality and debate? Little thought had been given to communicating the vision of the new institution to them.[5]

Another element in the educational mix was almost introduced when in November Premier Regan announced his government's decision for an eight-million-dollar move of the Adult Vocational Training Centre (AVTC) from its run-down buildings at Point Edward to the NSEIT-Xavier College campus for the fall of 1976. This opened the question as to its location on the campus and its relationship to the other facility, particularly the trades training component of NSEIT. Discussion with government indicated that while it might share some facilities with the other two, the nature of its programs indicated that it should be left separate, at least for the time being.[6]

Spared from having to deal with the AVTC as well, the Advisory Committee's executive had a free hand to continue its work on incorporation, using the Dalhousie and St. FX charters as models. The work coincided with the latter's appointment of a bylaws committee to examine, among other things, the concept of its affiliation with the new Sydney institution for degree-granting purposes.[7] The Advisory Committee, however, wanted degree-granting status for the new institution, and in its draft incorporation asserted, "The University shall have the power to grant degrees, diplomas and certificates but shall be affiliated for degree-granting purposes with Saint Francis Xavier University."[8]

For opponents of the new institution, the terms "university" and "power to grant degrees" were inflammatory. This was particularly the case for the town of Antigonish, which felt as if it were under siege, as the new College became a stronger possibility. Fears were also spreading in Antigonish that a much-needed new hospital would be located in Cape Breton, while a new shopping centre in Port Hawkesbury would further endanger its economy and mean a loss of business. Questions were asked as to why "Sullivan U" was getting so much support from DEVCO ("DEVCO College" was another term used), to the detriment of their region, while their powerful member of parliament, Allan J. MacEachen, seemed passive. They claimed that allowing the new college to be born would lead to a proliferation of degree-granting institutions—in Liverpool or Amherst, maybe—which would add to the declining enrolment that St. FX had experienced the previous year.[9]

Undaunted by such opposition, excitement began to mount in the Industrial Area as calls went out for a name for the new institution. The Rotary Club of North Sydney claimed that it should include the words "university" for prestige and "Cape Breton" (though others felt that name might hurt its reputation). Other suggested names poured into the committee, the most popular being "University of Cape Breton" or "Cape Breton University." Other names, such as "Cape Breton University of Arts and Technology," "Breton Polytechnical University" and "University College of Cape Breton," all finished far behind in popularity. The committee voted in favour of the "University of Cape Breton," with twelve votes for "University College of Cape Breton" as second choice. It was decided to keep the decision secret since the term "university" would only inflame the opposition when the act of incorporation was finally introduced.[10]

By spring, Campbell felt that a draft of the bill for the act of incorporation was ready to be sent to Allan Sullivan for vetting. A lobbying committee to represent the Advisory Committee was chosen at the same time. It included Guy MacLean, a Cape Bretoner who was Dean of Arts and Science at Dalhousie University, which turned out to be a far-sighted appointment.[11]

When Sullivan, now Attorney General, received the draft of the act, he asked that Campbell and Denne Burchell meet to discuss it with him, along with St. FX President Malcolm MacDonnell and J.J. MacDonald, its Dean of Science, Arthur Murphy, Chairman of the University Grants Committee, and William Gillis, then Minister of Education and MLA for Antigonish. The pressure that the Antigonish Community was putting on its University became apparent in the hardening of its attitude toward the terms of the act. As expected the St. FX representatives strongly opposed the name "University" instead of "College," since the new institution would not be granting its own degrees. Gillis went on to question the whole meaning of degree-granting status; after all, Xavier was already giving part-time degrees. Campbell felt this was just a ploy to delay incorporation, but gave in on the matter of the name while standing firm that the College be enabled to grant degrees albeit only in affiliation with

St. FX. It was agreed that in the case of any disagreement over the initiation of degree programs that an arbitrator be appointed from each side, with a third to be mutually agreed upon.[12]

For Campbell, the document was "politically expedient," with deep restrictions on the College's activities, and he expressed his unhappiness, hoping it could eventually be amended.[13] The committee's greatest fear was that tying the College to a traditional university by not allowing it to offer its own degrees, would stifle the innovation that lay at the heart of the new institution. Other restrictions included a very large Board of 36, of whom 12 were to be appointed by the Minister of Education and of whom two were to be from St. FX. Finally, the provision for an independent evaluation of proposed courses weakened the power of the institution, suggesting to some members that this was just what Antigonish wanted.[14]

As the day for the introduction of the bill approached, opposition forces gathered. From New Glasgow to Port Hawkesbury, fears about the nature of the new institution caused alarm. St. FX threw a special luncheon at Port Hawkesbury to tell 110 community leaders: "We're your university." Outspoken mayor William (Billy Joe) MacLean decried the waste of taxpayers' money on a new institution in the "former" Industrial Area as "illogical."[15] Some town councillors in Antigonish sought support from MLAs beyond northern Nova Scotia.[16]

Sullivan introduced the Bill of Incorporation on the 24th of June. It was immediately sent to the Law Amendments Committee where, as expected, opposition came from Tory members from Northern Nova Scotia and Port Hawkesbury. The most upsetting remarks, however, came from the president of Dalhousie University, Henry Hicks, who declared the creation of the College unjustifiable and extremely unwise.[17] Campbell was fearful of the bad publicity such remarks would bring upon the college, but was emboldened when St. FX President Rev. Malcolm MacDonnell, indicated that any risks the new College might pose to his University were subordinate to Cape Breton's right to have a post-secondary institution of its own.[18] He was supported by Guy MacLean,

Dean of Arts and Science at Dalhousie, who, as member of the Sydney lobbying team, bravely defied his president and supported the bill. The new College's representatives, John Terry, Denne Burchell, and Tom Jala in particular, fended off questions and protests. Sullivan's objectivity was put to the test while he conducted the hearings, as he fought to prevent a politically dangerous Cape Breton-Mainland rift from widening. In the end, political wisdom prevailed and the bill passed with no opposition.[19]

The final victory was sweet, but a severely restricted institution had been born. The offspring would be called the College of Cape Breton; its degrees being offered through its somewhat reluctant parent St. FX; it was not allowed to offer programs duplicating those of other universities and all new programs needed the approval of the Governor-in-Council; its board was heavy with representatives of government as well as representatives from the parent university.[20]

The College of Cape Breton came into existence July 1, 1974. As one commentator put it, "The new Cape Breton College is ordained, or doomed, to spend most of its conscious life avoiding the modern mortal sin of bureaucracy—duplication." He warned that the whole experiment could be a disaster if the College was unclear as to what it was trying to invent. The founders only knew they were inventing a new type of institution combining the humanities and technology in new degrees and diplomas, and "It will be linked in an active way to the various components of the community ... it will have to help Cape Bretoners in all age groups live with their community as best they can."[21] The interpretation of this role was to be the object of debate and interpretation for years to come.

For the moment, however, the practical operation of the new institution was of primary concern. A Board of Governors composed mainly of members of the Advisory Committee and chaired by Rev. Clarence Nicholson was appointed.[22] During the summer of 1974, John Terry and D.F. Campbell directed the operations of their respective campuses, with William Reid, former Dean of Studies at XJC, assuming academic responsibilities for the Sydney campus. All summer long meetings were

Fig. 6. Photo by Owen Fitzgerald. College of Cape Breton Technology and Trades campus, c1974. Courtesy Robert Morgan.

held at both campuses to make *ad hoc* operational decisions and avoid misunderstandings. As there was no comptroller yet appointed, the accounting firm of Touche Ross acted as financial advisors, drawing up operating budgets for the Sydney campus, as well as for the new College as a whole in preparation for presentation to the Maritime Provinces Higher Education Commission (MPHEC), the body which approved university courses in the region.[23]

An organizational committee held joint meetings of the two campus faculties in September to discuss the structure of the new College. The faculty of the tech campus had left the tutelage of the Department of Education to become employees of the College Board and new committees were needed for matters such as grievances, and rank and tenure for the academic employees. It was agreed to appoint a joint committee to prepare plans for objectives and policies as well as organization of the College, while retaining other committees until the new structure was adopted.[24]

Throughout the fall the Board and Organization Committee worked on an administrative structure adopted in December.[25] The first president was D.F. Campbell; Senior Vice-President Development was John Terry; William Reid was Academic Vice-President, to whom deans would report; and James Fleming became the first Director of Finance and Administration.[26] George Leith, a psychologist, formerly of the Universities of Birmingham, Memorial, and Utrecht, was appointed Dean of Arts and Science, replacing Reid in July, 1975.[27] In January an administrative council, consisting of the Senior Vice-President Development, Academic Vice-President, and the Director of Finance and Administration, was charged with the responsibility of the overall co-ordination of the College administration.[28] By spring, the Technology/Trades faculty's dean, Robert (Bob) Rudderham, was in place, as well as the coordinators of Trades Training programs, Engineering Technology and Business Technology.[29] In the absence of a College Senate—College Council, as it was later called—a Committee on Educational Policies and Programs, consisting of faculty representatives and administration and chaired by the president, which had been set up early in 1974, continued to function, screening new programs and procedures and reporting directly to the Board.[30]

There was certainly no shortage of plans for new programs. The unification of the academic and technological worlds in one institution sparked an explosion of new course designs. During the summer of 1975, the Programs Committee began the design of interdisciplinary courses, and visited institutions in Canada and the United States to investigate novel approaches and programs.[31] Some programs, such as Instrumental, Petroleum, Environmental and Ecological Technologies had received governmental approval before amalgamation and it was hoped to have these introduced to at least the diploma level by 1975. By Fall, work was underway on an innovative BA which the programs committee hoped to introduce to the St. Francis Xavier Senate for approval during the academic year. What eventually became the Bachelor of Arts Community Studies, the institution's first degree, arose from the need to be innovative and avoid duplicating other institutions' degrees. A committee combining both academic and technology faculty and administrators planned the degree to give students the opportunity to develop skills and to be made aware of how problems are analyzed and solved in the real world. The College's first degree was innovative in that it contained a "core curriculum," which all candidates had to take to ensure a well-grounded education.[32] A real fear was that not only would it not be accepted by traditional universities, but that even the College's academics would reject it. Eventually, George Leith, Dean of Arts and Science convinced his colleagues of its value, uniqueness and academic rigour.[33] The degree would not be inaugurated until 1975.

Literally dozens of other course plans were in various stages of preparation, such as communication arts, paralegal studies, museology, ethnic studies, public administration, hospitality, drafting technology, and courses for nursing, paramedical personnel, and other professionals. Campbell felt this outburst of educational creativity illustrated the value of the new college in opening additional options for students.[34]

These plans had to survive the harsh reality of Nova Scotia's academic and political world. Any degree programs needed the endorsement of St. Francis Xavier, then the MPHEC. There was worry that the latter and the influential Atlantic Association of University Academic Vice-Presidents did not have the appropriate background to evaluate many of the innovative programs, particularly technology. The young institution had little influence on the Association of Vice-Presidents; in fact it was not even a member. Nor was encouragement forthcoming. Arthur Murphy, Chairman of the University Grants Committee, discouraged the discussion of real innovation until the College was up and running. Even Sullivan discouraged the rush into new programs, and the ever careful William Gillis kept warning that CCB must stay within its budget.[35] By December, the innovative BA was under scrutiny by external assessors and the process was beginning to drag on.[36] Other courses approved by the board and still hanging fire were Para-legal Technology, and Engineering Studies.

Though the College had to battle external forces for course recognition, numerous internal innovations could be made, many in response to community needs. A Resource Learning Centre to make educational resources available to local teachers, an Electronic Learning Centre and a Reading and Writing Centre to boost entering students' literacy levels were introduced. Part-time credit programs enrolled 840 students with 51 courses offered in the evenings in 1974-75. Of the 35 non-credit courses offered that year 11 were new, dealing with everything from women and the law to confluent education and seminars for school librarians. Intersession courses, falling between winter and summer terms, were introduced in

1974 with four courses and an enrolment of 74. This was expanded in 1975 to 10 courses with an expected enrolment of 200. In fact, 454 registered.[37]

With the vast increase in new programs there was an obvious need for some internal mechanism to approve new courses and prepare documentation for presentation to the MPHEC. The earliest committee for internal program screening, a Committee on Educational Policies and Programs, had been established in early 1974; by May of that year, as it became clearer that the new college would be born, the Sydney campus endorsed the organization of a Senate, with representatives from faculty, administration, students, and the community.[38] Further discussions led to the idea of a unique "College Council," combining both advisory and academic functions.

This was a compromise between the current unicameral operation and a bicameral one which would strictly divide powers between the board and a Senate, typical in other colleges. A council allowed inputs from various levels including the board, which would have faculty, community and student representation along with administration. By October, 1976 it was agreed: "The College Council would become an educational body concerned with determining and overseeing educational matters and recommending certain educational priorities."[39] By the fall of 1976, by-laws were agreed upon and approved by the board. The early idea of the president as chair was scrapped before the first meeting of the council December 15, 1976 when Prof. Charles MacDonald presided.[40] It was not long before the growing demands on the Council led to the establishment of council committees concerned with objectives, programs, academics, the campus, and nominations.[41] In January 1980, its membership became firm at 35, with the Registrar as a new member *ex officio*, together with other administrative representatives, including the president, deans, senior vice-president, and academic vice-president.[42]

The development of the College Council brought greater input of faculty into program selection. In fact, it became a debating arena over the nature of the College. Though the College's mandate was innovation, as in the case of the BA, some academics were skeptical about the offering of less traditional college programs. There was great suspicion, for example, toward the offering of Speech Communication, a program not offered elsewhere but avidly promoted by Mary Lynch. Many opposed this non-traditional program, even though the College had "staked its claim" to it with the MPHEC.[43] No move was made to proceed on the implementation of the program until, finally in 1981, the Faculty of Arts and Science debated its academic worth, giving it very lukewarm support.[44] This had the effect of greatly weakening the commitment to the program and Lynch suggested the College release its hold on the program to allow other universities to adopt it.[45] Though the council was unwilling to do that, Speech Communication was not recognized as an academic subject until 1983.[46]

Another area that upset many traditional academics was Continuing Education. This department was under the jurisdiction of the Senior Vice-President, while the traditional academic programs were under the Dean of Arts and Sciences. Continuing Education extended back to the very reason for the establishment of the Junior College: to be a source of community education so that teachers, or even people with little formal education, could take courses to improve themselves. Numerous courses were accordingly being offered on a part-time basis in both credit and non-credit areas, many of which, like fiddling, step dancing or even studies in more traditional fields like literature or history drew considerable numbers. In 1974-75 for example, 1,178 people were taking non-credit courses in comparison to 537 in Arts and Science and 513 in Technology and Trades.[47] This led a number of academics to fear that the part-time "credit-free" courses were draining students from their courses. Discussion at College Council centred around the desirability of "getting back to traditional Liberal arts courses rather than putting so much emphasis on innovative courses."[48] There were allegations that courses offered by Continuing Education were easier, and since different administrators had jurisdiction over part-time and traditional academic courses, rivalries and redundancies were being created.

In order to stem the tide of problems, it was decided that Ora McManus, Director of Continuing Education, should undertake a study of the department. He reported that his group would like more community-based programs, especially those interfacing with local industry for community development. He noted that the non-degree courses drew students to the College, which helped support Continuing Education since the MPHEC gave no financial aid to the college for these courses. Everyone agreed that a policy was needed to govern the relationship between Continuing Education and the various faculties. A Board committee was appointed to draw up a strategy to address this and send it to College Council for debate.[49] The committee suggested that Continuing Education be placed under the jurisdiction of the Academic Vice-President and that the deans of the appropriate faculties assume responsibility for academic courses that had been undertaken by Continuing Education. This sparked a heated debate; words like "power grab" and "paranoia" were hurled back and forth, but the issue highlighted the new college's dilemma over innovation, academic respectability and community development.[50]

Like Continuing Education, the institutes also enjoyed considerable autonomy. The organization of institutes dated from the Junior College's attempt to stimulate community-based research and expertise in a college lacking graduate students. The first three institutes, the Bras d'Or, the Beaton Institute of Cape Breton Studies and the Tompkins Institute for Human Values and Technology, were formally organized in 1975, followed by the Centre for International Studies in 1978.

The Bras d'Or Institute, under the direction of Donald Arseneau, Professor of Chemistry, was, in effect, precursor of the Department of Research and Development. The Institute's aim was to undertake research projects of importance to Cape Breton, not only in science, such as aquaculture and coal research, but social issues such as housing. As Arseneau prophetically put it, "What is cheaper to ship than information?"[51] The Bras d'Or Institute launched the college's first conferences and seminars, such as an Aquaculture Conference July 17-20, 1975, which attracted 200 participants.[52] A spin-off from the Institute was New Dawn Enterprises, a unique community economic development body.[53] The Bras d'Or Institute also planned the development of the Atlantic Coal Institute, which was organized in 1980, eventually receiving the College's first large research funds, for work on coal analysis, carbogel and fluidized bed combustion for the coal industry. Arseneau and Ora McManus led the development of the Coal Institute which, in 1983, received a million dollars to open a laboratory at the Adult Vocational Training Centre under the directorship of Dieter Birk.[54]

The Beaton Institute had began with the work of the XJC pioneer librarian, the energetic and greatly-loved Sister St. Margaret of Scotland, CND, later Sister Margaret Beaton, who had started to collect otherwise lost documents pertaining to Cape Breton history. She called her collection "Cape Bretoniana." Sister Beaton's interest in the collection led her to leave the library to assume full-time operation of Cape Bretoniana. As the collection grew, there was a constant search for space, first at MacLeod House on Nepean Street, then at the Logue Building, a former automobile showroom. The tragic death of Sister Beaton at age 81 in an automobile accident June 12, 1975, left the operation under the interim direction of the College's former principal, the ever-loyal and dedicated Dr. Malcolm MacLellan, with the help of Hilda Day, Sister Beaton's respected assistant and font of all things Cape Breton. In that same year, Cape Bretoniana was renamed the Beaton Institute with a mandate to collect and research the social, cultural, ethnic and folk history to the island. In 1976, the now important collection of hundreds of tapes and thousands of manuscripts, maps and photos came under the direction of Robert Morgan, until his retirement in 2001. The Institute is recognized as one of Canada's leading regional archives, has stimulated considerable research and scholarly publication and is a source for local folklore, genealogical information and student research.[55]

The Humanitechnical Institute was established to deal with the relationships between technology and the humanities, and the impact of technological change on society. The name was changed in 1974 to the Tompkins Institute, reflecting the great work of Rev. Jimmy Tompkins in human development in Cape Breton earlier in the 20th century.[56] It was an ideal institute for the College, since it sought to unify learning and to link social reform with the world of technology. It was hoped that the intellectual inquiry this spawned would bring the College not only into the development of the community, but give it academic respectability.[57] Peter Dawson, the Chair of the Philosophy Department at Memorial University came as director to be followed by Marcel LeRoy and by Rev. Greg MacLeod, who involved the Institute not only in academic research, but in innovative community development so deeply rooted in the region's social inheritance.

The final early institute funded by the College was the Centre for International Studies, the first devoted to international studies at an undergraduate institution in Canada. Founded in 1978 and headed by Brian Tennyson of the History Department, the Institute was soon involved in working with developing countries, providing job training in places like The Gambia. Proof of the valuable work of the Institute came in 1981, when it received a $216,000 grant from the Canadian International Development Agency to help the College work with the World Bank to send instructors to the Gambia Technical Institute. It is interesting that the work involved the co-operation of Tennyson and George Brown, the Coordinator of Trades Training, indicating the potential for the useful combination for trades and academics in College projects.[58]

This Institute was also invaluable in bringing foreign students to the College. After years of attempts, Tennyson finally managed to have the College Council set up a Committee on Foreign Students to investigate such a program. Though the College had received individual students from places like Nigeria and Libya, it planned to approach the subject in a more organized manner with a three-percent target for foreign-student enrolment. Part of the support for this project came from those who hoped that expected declining enrolments later in the 80s could be at least partially offset by foreign students.[59]

Like Continuing Education and the Institutes, whose development responded to peculiar local concerns, Trades training within the College was also unique. Unlike the vocational training which took place at the AVTC, Trades training at CCB was basically apprenticeship training for those already employed and, as such, had been an integral part of the NSEIT. With the formation of the new campus, the College replaced the Department of Education, working with the Department of Labour in organizing courses and training schedules. Soon all of DEVCO's training programs were centralized within the College and the programs seemed to be working well.[60] By 1978, however, problems were arising with the provincially regulated apprenticeship training allocated for CCB students.[61]

Generally, students undertaking apprenticeship training between Truro and Sydney studied at CCB, with their funding based on the number of training days allotted to the training institution. Because all funding came directly from the Department of Labour, the College could not budget for any changes in the number of training days it was allocated. Hence, when in the late 1970s training days were cut and training boundaries were changed, allocating students in New Glasgow to Halifax with no input from the College, fears as to the future of the apprenticeship program at CCB were raised.[62] Sullivan and Campbell managed to convince the Minister of Labour to reimburse the College for those losses for 1978-80 and to increase the money allocated per training day. In the meantime, a special Trades Committee was appointed to develop new programs.[63] The upshot of this was new programs for the fishing industry and the training of technicians in the offshore.[64]

Despite these changes, the government continued cutting programs and training days in Cape Breton, while reducing CCB's training catchment area from New Glasgow to Antigonish, which resulted in the layoff of instructors.[65] These cuts resulted in new courses originally planned for Sydney being transferred to Halifax. By 1983, four classes were closed indicating a need for more regular contact with government bureaucrats. However, this brought little satisfaction as growing unemployment in Cape Breton meant the loss of students; only employed people could undertake apprenticeship training. In an attempt to broaden the student base, the Apprenticeship Training Committee was renamed the "Training Committee" in 1983, but the whole program faced serious challenges as the number of students per class fell from an average of 22-24 to 8-10 in 1984.[66]

Throughout this period of academic development and controversy, the College had to wrestle with the relocation of the campus. In November 1973, the college commissioned the firm of F.W. Woodcock and Associates of Toronto to begin master planning studies based on space requirements and shared facilities to accommodate the former Xavier College campus, NSEIT and the AVTC. From the very beginning, Woodcock ignored the latter in estimates, due largely to the distance of its Point Edward location from the NSEIT. They came up with a plan for 53,695 square metres (577,968 square feet) of new space in addition to 18,580 square metres of alterations to the NSEIT campus. Individual buildings included a campus centre/theatre (10,725 square metres) with an arts and sciences centre (16,590), an academic wing (5,786), an 845 square metre library, an athletic centre (8,750) and an ice arena (2,630)—$20,185,606 in new construction. When added to the planned-for alterations to NSEIT and property development, including water supply, roads, parking, playing fields, tennis courts, landscaping and fees, the anticipated price tag was $26,418,745. With inflation running rampant at the time a 10-percent cost-allocation clause was added, to bring the gross total to $30,777,838.[67] The advisory committee, forerunner of the College's Board of Governors, accepted the proposal and moved to hire a project manager and organize a campus development committee of the Board for site preparation. [68] The College was under pressure to move since it had been informed by St. FX in June that, as of July 1, 1974, their fiscal responsibilities for the downtown campus would cease.[69]

The rapid move to a new campus was a dream project. Like the great plans for exciting new courses, this dream too would be whittled down and predictably delayed by government before coming to fruition, at an even greater cost to the taxpayer, more than two decades later.

The Treasury Board rejected the cost and William Gillis, the Minister of Education, informed Campbell that the College would get only $12,000,000, requested a new plan based on that amount and told him not to make a move before each individual project component was approved.[70] A flurry of meetings took place between Woodcock, the Board, Gillis, and Allan Sullivan, during which matters grew even worse. The

Board was told the $12,000,000 *included* escalation, infrastructure and consulting fees; new space was strictly limited to Lauwreys' recommendations of 22,575 square metres (243,000 square feet).[71]

The Campus Planning Committee, also called the Space Planning Committee, had no choice but to make drastic cuts. The library was first to be sacrificed, cut back to 7,430 square metres and all the other centres suffered accordingly.[72] Because radical changes would have to be made in their planning concepts, Woodcock would have to undertake detailed planning in Halifax, rather than Toronto, so as to be near the centralized government bureaucrats. Because the firm could not accommodate such an arrangement, they were let go. A new approach was needed quickly and, in April 1974, the Board hired Nova Scotia architects, Duffus, Romans, Kudzins, Rounsefell.[73]

Their first attempt slashed non-existent (though wished-for) facilities by seventy percent and left part of the campus in downtown Sydney, with a view of gradually moving it all to the NSEIT site. Parts of the campus left in Sydney would include the science faculty offices, the Student Centre at the Lyceum, and administration offices for both campuses, which in January had been centralized in the former Westminster Church on George Street.[74] Other space, such as the Logue Building and MacLeod House, would be evaluated. This plan would leave 12,350 square metres of space to be developed first on the new campus, well below the 21,460 square metres that Lauwreys and the government had once agreed was adequate. However, the total cost for the 12,350 square metres was just under $12 million, the fiscal ceiling allotted by the education and finance powers-that-be in Halifax.

Campbell warned that this arrangement would split the campus, endangering the integration of facilities and personnel.[75] The plan was deemed unworkable and, in August, Education Minister Gillis was quoted as saying it was in "limbo" and he decided to move the whole problem to the doorstep of the MPHEC, fretting to the press that he had "grave concerns" about the project and that work would not get underway on the new campus during 1975.[76] This may have been said with secret relief, since rampant inflation at the time was eating into the province's budget to the extent that he feared a cut of thirty-five percent in the College's operating budget for the next academic year.[77]

Gillis's statements to the press angered the board who felt he was putting the future of the College in a poor light and intensifying negative attitudes toward Cape Breton on the part of Halifax press and Mainland universities. He was asked to refrain from making press statements. At first, he adamantly refused, but finally agreed to a press release indicating that the College Board had acted conscientiously in its expansion plans and that "the commitment ... by the government of Nova Scotia with regard to the establishment of the College is in no way affected by the decision to refer the matter to the Maritime Provinces Higher Education Commission."[78]

Within two months, the MPHEC and the province came up with 16 million dollars for the new campus, which, while still short, caused the exhausted but realistic Campbell to advise acceptance, to "get on with the job" of building an "adequate" facility.[79] The amount set aside for buildings was $13.1 million, with new equipment costing $2.3 million. This would give 14,865 square metres (160,000 square feet) of new floor space and 4,645 square metres of modified space in the original buildings.[80] The administration, while not entirely happy, uttered things like "it is better to have too little space than too much," or that an expected drop in enrolment in the 1980s would lessen the space needs.[81]

In reality, the project was full of pitfalls. Costs did not include provision for inflation which was escalating rapidly at the time; indeed, estimates were made (in May-1975 dollars) with only a vague provision for adjustments.[82] A master plan was drawn up dividing the construction into four phases, most of which were undertaken simultaneously. Phase I included the athletic and recreation centre; phase II, the campus centre including the cafeteria, multi-purpose rooms (later a faculty and student lounge, classrooms, and offices); phase III, an information centre, including the Library and the Beaton Institute, theatre, main entrance, art gallery, and president's office area including the boardroom (today a children's day care area); phase IV, alterations to the "A" Wing South, and "B" Block which at the time was the NSEIT gymnasium.[83] All buildings were linked for ease of access. The plan was completed by December and was approved by the board and MPHEC by March 1974. Leonard Chiasson, PEng, was appointed Project Coordinator and specifications were immediately begun for a 745 square metre (8,000 square foot) extension to the "C" Wing.[84] This was completed in November, just after the official sod-turning, which was held October 28 when Campbell led a group of 350 staff and students to a spot bright with autumn leaves near the Glace Bay entrance to the campus for a sweetgrass ceremony performed by Mi'kmaq Grand Chief Donald Marshall.

The College was now caught up in construction fever. In July, $547,000 was approved for renovations to the "A" Wing. As they began it was noted that the original estimates for this project, made less than two years previously, had totaled $400,000, but that inflation had increased costs despite reductions in the original plans. Further cuts were impossible; as it was, the College was left with an inadequate facility which would hinder its scientific research potential for years to come.[85]

Seeing the problems inflation was causing, John Terry felt that instead of cutting back on buildings, which would only make them more inadequate, the Board should approach the MPHEC for more funding, noting that provision had been made for this.[86] He thought $15.7 million, as opposed to the allotted $13.1 million, would be needed to complete the buildings.[87] Campbell had expressed his fears to Catherine Wallace, chair of the MPHEC, writing, "My concern now ... is that in trying to achieve this objective [adequate facilities at the lowest possible cost] within the estimates based on 1975 dollars we are cutting back on design features which will result in facilities that will be inadequate, inefficient, and in the long term uneconomic....[88] Still the MPHEC did not agree to new funding.[89]

As a result, cuts in quality began. In 1977, lower cost materials were used in glazing of the study carrels and skylights, a decision that would plague the library for years to come. Cheaper ceiling materials were used and still costs increased from the $14.24 million estimates of 1975 to $15.69 million in 1977-78.[90] Inflation meant that the original estimate of $645 per square metre for new buildings was now $700, on a par with St. FX's new science buildings and Acadia's new arts building ($785 per square metre).[91] In 1978, with still no budgetary help in sight, plans for landscaping were abandoned and window sizes changed.[92]

Despite frustration and misgivings, plans could not be abandoned. The federal Department of Public Works which had bought the Arts and Science buildings in Sydney wanted to take possession in July 1979, meaning the library at the new campus would have to be ready at that time. As well, the pressure was mounting since the Beaton Institute had left the Logue Building after a fire broke out endangering its collection there. It was temporarily housed in a former car painting facility at the AVTC. As well, the Student Union area in the Lyceum was having maintenance problems and could not be properly repaired since all non-space money had been allocated to the new buildings.[93]

Finally, in June 1979, a further $900,000 was approved by the government.[94] By the summer, the library was completed and the move was underway, a gigantic task next to which all the other moves paled.[95] All employees were on campus by October and classes were underway in rooms barely completed. Indeed, the rush and the cuts had left a long legacy of problems. As John Terry explained, an occupant does not normally move in or accept a new building until deficiencies are cleared up, but the College was forced to move in as various phases of construction were completed and before deficiencies could be properly eliminated. Though staff and students were soon complaining about inadequacies, Terry felt only time would help clear these up and suggested that a positive message be put out so as not to mar the image of the College.[96] A long struggle ensued with the construction management services company to correct problems.[97]

The final tally of construction costs continued to trickle in for at least four years after occupancy. Construction costs by October 1981 were at $17,319,397; government agreed to pay all but $289,000, of which

$100,000 was interest charges. Cost overruns, which eventually amounted to $508,000 were only two percent of total costs, which was surprising in an inflationary era, and perhaps indicate savings that hurt the fabric of the buildings.[98] Finally, in 1983, the government agreed to pay a number of outstanding amounts from the construction period.[99]

Fig. 7. Photo by Owen Fitzgerald. College of Cape Breton under construction, c1977. Beaton Institute of Cape Breton Studies, University College of Cape Breton. 78-131-1881.

Even before the new building, meant to accommodate 1,200, was completed, it was inadequate to house the growing numbers of students and staff, for despite dire predictions of falling birth rates and fewer people attending university, student enrolment showed a steady increase. At the time of amalgamation in 1974, full-time enrolment numbered 1083, with 587 in arts and science, 141 in trades, 372 in technology, 840 part time and 742 at summer school. The latter number included those attending the College of Cape Breton's first intersession in May-June, 1974, the largest summer school ever held on the Island.[100] Though the phenomenon of new student enrolment increases were partly offset by students leaving after one year to complete their studies "away," it was becoming apparent by 1975, that new courses, such as the Bachelor of Arts Community Studies were beginning to draw new students, offsetting the loss.[101] Indeed, full time enrolment was 214 higher than 1974, with technology programs fully enrolled.[102]

It was at this point that the MPHEC, with plans for College expansion already in the air, began to wonder about its growth patterns. Sister Catherine Wallace, Chair of the MPHEC, had a member of her staff, Helmut Schweiger, visit Sydney to meet the registrar, Donald Fewer, to discuss his projected enrolment of 1,600 by 1980. Schweiger disagreed with this estimate and took the message back to Wallace that he expected there would be only 1,200 students enrolled at the College by then. Though the college administrators disagreed with Schweiger's figures to the point of "incredibility," his figures were accepted by the MPHEC, with the result that the new building was almost immediately inadequate.[103]

Still, the fear of falling birth rates haunted all centres of higher learning at the time. In Cape Breton out-migration and poor economic conditions seemed to compound the problem. In the fall of 1976, full-time enrolment was up by only two percent, to 1,212.[104] Realizing that students were becoming more mobile and interested in residences, and that the image of the College, which was still on two campuses and in inadequate quarters, was poor, it was decided that serious recruitment must be undertaken. Student participation rates in Cape Breton County were well below the national average, with young men still being lured by jobs in the mines and steel plant.[105] The recruitment drive and new publicity paid off, with student applications up thirty-six percent for technology and twenty-four percent for arts and science over the previous year[106]—1978 enrolment showed an overall increase of five percent.[107]

The last year of the dual campus, 1979, saw a decline in registration of both incoming and returning students totalling seven percent. Donald Fewer believed that the College's main drawback was its lack of a residence, but that the message of a new campus was getting out and might change the situation. Interestingly, off-island applications rose in 1979, though ninety-five percent of students still came from Cape Breton, with technology students at seventy-five percent.

The 1979 decrease led to changes in the approach to recruitment. A recruiting officer was hired and high school students were brought to see the newly opened facilities. The scholarship program was extended by an additional sixty thousand dollars, thanks to the kind donation of Bruce and Dorothy Rosetti of Sydney.[108] The results were startling. The number of full-time students rose seven percent over 1979 to 1,184, with 830 part time.[109] In his annual report, Campbell noted, however, that part-time enrolment had been decreasing steadily in the past four years, since in order to improve their licenses with graduate studies, teachers had to go to graduate universities. As a result, he was trying to convince the Minister of Education to allow the College to offer graduate programs to teachers.[110]

The trend of increasing enrolments continued during the early 1980s, confounding MPHEC expectations and placing heavy strains on the limited space at the college. A prime reason behind the increases was that, despite a declining birth rate, more people between the ages of 18 and 24, especially women, were beginning to attend university as educational requirements rose in the workplace. This was particularly true in technology which was attracting increasing numbers of Mainland candidates. By 1981, full-time enrolment reached the crucial 1200 figure, with Continuing Education numbers at 800, and technology at 500, which included engineering and business.[111] The following year, arts, science, and technology rose sharply to 1,481 in response to increasing unemployment in the area, the rising expense of studying elsewhere, the degree-granting status that had been acquired that year and the development of the College infrastructure, making it more attractive to students.

The increasing numbers highlighted the overcrowding and clutter in the halls. The grounds were neglected and unattractive due to cuts in landscaping expenditures. The condition of the campus was causing embarrassment.[112] Worse still was lack of classrooms for the growing number of courses. It was considered that 19 new classrooms were needed. And because government restraint precluded the addition of more, alternative space was sought out at the AVTC.[113] Projections had predicted a base enrolment of 1,200 by 1990, but 1984 figures—temporarily as it proved—levelled out at about 1,900 students.[114]

The rapid growth of the College, the location on the new campus and the unique blending of academic and technology studies called for new symbols and sense of identity apart from that of the founding institutions. The challenge was highlighted by some technology students' wanting their diplomas issued by NSEIT when the idea of a single diploma was introduced in 1974. It was decided to avoid heavy-handedness, and a compromise was reached which allowed the use of both names on the diplomas for that year. The first graduation, held May 11, 1975 at the technology campus, was addressed by the admired "voice of Cape Breton," Ann Terry MacLellan, who appropriately stressed the fact that great visionaries were practical people who knew how to dream and translate those dreams and visions into practical reality.[115]

Earlier that month, the Board of Governors approved a seal reading "College of Cape Breton, established June 28, 1974" and set up a College-wide committee to study a logo and coat-of-arms.[116] In order to stir student interest in the process a prize was offered to anyone coming up with the winning logo, which was finally won by Steven Zwarun of Glace Bay.[117] Meanwhile, in March 1976, the college colours of white, Kelly green, and Texas orange were adopted, along with the appropriately predictable team name "Capers."[118]

The following year, a design for the coat-of-arms was approved. The design was crested by a Canterbury Cap and a cluster of mayflowers, beneath which was the logo over a sprig of spruce, representing the native population. A Cape Breton sloop, taken from the seal of the Colony of Cape Breton, was below this.[119] Many of the ideas for the coat-of-arms came from James Lovelace of Sydney, who had designed Sydney's recently updated coat-of-arms.

A potentially embarrassing moment, though humorous in retrospect, occurred when it came to the adoption of a college motto. The executive of the board chose the rather bland "*Veritas Vincit*," ("truth conquers") from 23 mottoes presented by the logo and coat-of-arms committee, with the runner-up "Achieve Patiently," which perhaps reflected the mood of many at the College at the time. Unfortunately, the first choice had to be scrapped when it was discovered that it was the motto of a Halifax brewery.[120] The following year the committee undertook its task afresh and submitted the motto "To Follow Wisdom."[121] This choice was hotly debated and the idea of translating it into Gaelic came up. If this was the case, something more original should be used, so that motto was tossed aside and everyone agreed with Campbell to ask Norman MacDonald, professor of Gaelic Studies to look into a suitable motto. Two months later MacDonald recommended "*Theid Dichioll Air Thoisead*," which roughly translated means "Diligence Triumphs Over All" or "Extreme Perseverance Brings Best Results." MacDonald rightfully explained that, given its history, the motto had real meaning both for the College and for Cape Breton. The board approved the motto April 25, 1980.[122]

Other symbols of the College appeared in the next few years. The college mascot, "Chiever" the Cape Breton beaver, was adopted in 1981, representing a symbol of Canada. The name "Chiever" referred to an achiever who set goals to achieve at the College.[123] A tartan, designed by Patsy MacMullin, and based on the college colours, and an academic gown for the president came into existence in 1983.[124]

SYMBOLS ASIDE, UNITY was slow in coming, and only mutual respect and a unified sense of purpose could bring it about. Debate over having one or two graduations continued into the 80s, arts and sciences favouring two, though the administration held to one, as most students appeared at the ever- lengthening ceremony.[125] The first graduation on the new campus, June 21, 1980, brought together for the first time all the faculties in their new home. Bishop Power of Antigonish addressed the convocation, calling the union of the disciplines, a "marriage."[126]

When the move to the new campus was completed, another step toward unity came when respective Student Unions were combined into one body.[127] The students were allowed to find their own way which, while encouraging independence of thought, left them with little guidance. They held popular "beer bashes," which resulted in property and indeed human damage, as well as "misplaced" money and liquor stock—student accounts did not go through the College treasurer, and books were poorly maintained. As the Union was responsible for damages and financial losses, the result was an Advisory Council which helped the students operate in a responsible manner so that by 1980, all was in "good order."[128]

Another landmark for student activity of the early 80s was the founding of the *Caper Chronicle* in 1981, the student newspaper/journal, funded by the Student Union, and an Honours Society, "*Na Gaisgech*," "The Heroes," or "The Achievers," to draw attention to academic excellence.[129] One student group which drew the interest of the community was the drama group and their Festival of Plays, which had begun in 1971 and continued into the new institution and, in fact, to this day. From humble beginnings under Elizabeth and Harry Boardmore, the Festival became a regional attraction when it moved into the new campus playhouse, later named in their honour. Such activities not only united the College, drawing participation from all sectors, but involved the community in the life of the institution.

The launching of the College of Cape Breton Press, a daring and unique venture by President Campbell in 1974, brought the College to the community even more. Its first publication, *Patterson's History of Victoria County*, set the important local character of the press. It produced not only books, but best-selling record albums featuring Cape Breton talent: *Glendale 77* and the *Rise and Follies of Cape Breton*, two landmarks in the renaissance of Cape Breton culture that accompanied the birth of the College. Historical maps followed, and conference papers. The College's role in the life of its community was becoming established during this period.[130]

Athletics likewise united the institution to the community. Until this time growth had been slow but steady. Carl "Bucky" Buchanan had been hired as Director of Athletics in 1968, and in 1969 a gymnastics club had been organized. It was a model of the *community*-university concept with parents deeply involved in its operation. In the following years, the College produced the most successful sports teams in the Nova Scotia College Conference, with 32 team championships. By 1974, the institution hosted the Canadian College Association Championships, eventually winning the Canadian College volleyball championship in 1981. With the 1981 move to the superb Sullivan Field House, largely designed by Buchanan, Jack Porter, Russell MacNeil, and Frank MacNamara, students could finally enjoy long-needed sport facilities. Results were quick in coming—in 1982 the College won the Nova Scotia College Championships in men's volleyball, women's basketball, co-ed badminton and men's soccer. As well, the Capers hockey team won the Maritime Conference championship.[131]

With the final approval of the BA, 1982 was a key year academically. The 1974 incorporation of the College had specified that all degrees were to be offered through St. FX. But by 1981, with the new campus and rapid growth, as well as the parent university's final realization that the College was no real threat to its own existence, it became apparent to everyone that this anomaly must end. College administrators met with the premier on this topic in February of that year and received a favourable reply. They supplied him with arguments in favour of the degree-granting status to bring to Cabinet, and decided on a low-key approach featuring a media campaign emphasizing the positive advantages of the change.[132] St. FX fell in line, saying they would not oppose the College's independent degree-granting status.[133] The result was a meeting with the Minister of Education in January 1982, to amend the College Act allowing degree-granting autonomy. The proposed bill amending the Act of Incorporation was mentioned in the speech from the throne and a smooth passage was expected.[134] The Act was duly introduced and the College's Bylaws Committee began working on the revisions, which also meant lowering Board of Governors' membership from 38 to 36, with the withdrawal of the mandatory two St. FX representatives, eventually adding a chancellor and agreeing to the new name, "University College of Cape Breton," in recognition of the combination of the technology (diploma-granting) and academic (degree-granting) aspects of the institution.[135] By June 1 the committee had completed the work and a bill was sent to the legislature for introduction June 14, 1982. But there was another catch. This time the government wanted to have new programs approved by the MPHEC. Board members pressured Premier Buchanan to rescind this, which he agreed to do, but he could not prevent programs being approved by Cabinet, probably at the insistence of Ministers representing other university constituencies. With this partial victory, and fearing the loss or delay of the whole project, it was decided to let the Act stand.[136] It received royal assent June 26, 1982, and the first fully independent University College of Cape Breton degrees were awarded in June 1983.

After years of mind-numbing struggle, the College had finally achieved its dream of a full-time BA and a new campus. Its first president had inherited a small college of a few hundred students and, with the Board, faculty, students and community had built a growing, innovative University College with a hopeful future. This in a community facing deep economic insecurity. Campbell, anticipating or at least hoping for these outcomes, had informed the Board of his intention not to re-offer as president in June of 1982. He said he was leaving the post with "great personal satisfaction" and, like a true academic, would go back to teaching. A new president was to be chosen by June 30,1983.[137] His Board gave him a standing ovation and in an emotional moment, he commented that he hoped "that through the people with whom [I have worked], the College will continue to improve and grow."[138] The second era in the history of Cape Breton's centre of higher learning had come to a brilliant, if exhausting, conclusion.

V

The Turmoil of Growth, 1983-1989

During the six years beginning in 1983, the University College of Cape Breton entered another period of stress, one that threatened its very future. Though the economy of Industrial Cape Breton declined, full-time enrolment at UCCB more than doubled, resulting in serious overcrowding. While facilities deteriorated, morale sank and the structure of the institution began to creak. As an organization set up to meet the needs of a small college, it could not cope with the addition of new programs, underfunding and changing student and faculty attitudes. The inability of the University College to pry funding from cost-cutting governments fostered conflict between the administration and the Board and a deep and growing division between administration and faculty. The Canada Winter Games (1987) held largely at the University College brought about a great deal of interaction with the community, but could not make up for the institution's physical isolation, and the wrangling

Fig. 8. University College of Cape Breton, 1985. Beaton Institute of Cape Breton Studies, University College of Cape Breton. 97-621-28469.

over costs of the Games fed into open financial and administrative turmoil which boded ill for the future.

MUCH OF THE STRESS during these years fell on the shoulders of the University College's second president, William Maurice Reid. He seemed an admirable selection, as he had participated in the growth of the institution from junior college to the verge of full university status. A native of Quebec City, he had joined the physics department of St. Francis Xavier in 1949, but transferred to XJC in 1953. He became a full professor in 1962 and eight years later entered administration, first as Dean of Studies and finally, in 1974, as Academic Vice-President. His appointment in 1983, which he earnestly sought (but often later regretted), was seen as a bridge between the old and the new, the clerical to the lay president.[1] With his popular wife, Coleen "Dixie" Geldert, and five children, he brought a secular presence to what had seemed to many a clerically dominated college.

Reid was to lead a rapidly evolving institution. Despite falling birthrates, enrolment increased as more women entered college, high local unemployment invited people to improve their qualifications, studying "away" was becoming more expensive and imaginative new programs were introduced as a result of the new university status. The upshot was a physical plant burdened with twice the number of students for which it was designed. In 1983 alone, full-time student enrolment jumped by 30 percent to 1,500 students. Though increases were not nearly as dramatic in the ensuing years, continued high unemployment and the introduction of the BA helped enrolment spiral upward to 2,300 full-time students in September 1990 and to 2,500, with an additional 900 part-time students in 1992.[2] Off-campus programs also grew; by 1987 the Division of Continuing Studies was serving 2,000 students per year.[3]

Most enrolment remained local. In 1982, for example, only about 25 students came from off-island, a number which remained fairly static.[4] To diversify enrolment and enrich local students' educational experience further, plans were again developed to attract foreign students. Some Nigerian and Libyan students had occasionally attended the College, but the Centre for International Studies called for a target of three percent or 50 foreign students per year, for courses in English as a second language, and for pre-technical studies upgrading. Differential fees for foreign students were levied but dropped in 1990 (the fee later resumed).[5] Meanwhile the Centre received considerable funding from the Canadian International Development Agency (CIDA), allowing it to send instructors to The Gambia and, for 12 years beginning in 1983, to operate an office in downtown Sydney, which included resources for schools, workshops, and conferences.[6]

Though it was widely hoped that increased international student enrolment would bolster predicted falling enrolment, local registration remained strong during the decade. As a result, though off-island student numbers grew slowly, enrolment remained overwhelmingly local. Among local students there was an increasing number of Mi'kmaq. Prior to 1984, only three native students had graduated from the institution; only nine in 1985. Concern over these low numbers led Greg MacLeod of the Philosophy Department to approach Sister Dorothy Moore, herself Mi'kmaw, to rectify the situation. She volunteered one day per week, eventually working full-time, to initiate "native" studies courses—later more properly called Mi'kmaq Studies. Academic counselling programs, and an increase to eight full-credit and four cross-listed courses in Mik'maq lead to a tenfold increase in enrolment between 1984 and 1991, with three full-time and one part-time faculty. At first plagued by high drop-out rates, by 1990, 81.4 percent of native students enrolling remained at the institution, and some were heading for post-graduate studies.[7]

In 1990, the Humanities Department inaugurated the Mi'kmaq Studies sub-department. By 1991-92, with enrolment at 105 full-time, and 45 part-time Mi'kmaq students, native leaders and the University College were developing a plan for a more institutionalized native presence. Led by Charles MacDonald of the Humanities Department and Murdena Marshall, director of the Mi'kmaq Studies sub-department, an innovative Mi'kmaq Studies program was introduced, with courses such as Mi'kmaq for native and non-native speakers, Mi'kmaq history, linguistics, treaty rights, and the first tribal studies university program in Canada, all geared to the modern needs of the Mi'kmaq. Many of these programs were integrated into the humanities core courses. As a result, natives felt less alienated and now 80 percent of those entering the program were graduating.[8]

It seemed only natural that UCCB should pioneer in Mik'maq studies given the large number of native people on the island and the innovative nature of the institution. The province's political masters had agreed to its birth only if it be innovative and avoid costly course duplication with Mainland universities who in their turn feared competition. Enforced creativity thus became both life blood and Achilles heel—a number of academics still feared the sacrifice of traditional scholastic respectability to innovation. It took a decade for an innovative program like Speech Communication to overcome internal opposition before receiving academic recognition.[9] At the same time, however, the MPHEC was more used to dealing with approvals for traditional courses, and their slow approval of UCCB course proposals continually hampered the institution's attempt to introduce innovative programs. Some barriers were lifted when, in 1983, the MPHEC gave UCCB authority to modify existing programs without their approval.[10]

Within a few weeks of this breakthrough, moves were made to modify the existing BA by adding "core curriculum" courses that all students in the program must follow. Although this was unusual, it received formal provincial approval in less than two years, an unusually short period of time for approval of UCCB programs.[11] Still there were restrictions: the degree could be given only in courses where resources were adequate. Forbidden areas were economics, French, biochemistry, and speech communication.[12]

Newer programs were less fortunate. The MPHEC rejected plans for a Bachelor of Science degree in Business Administration because they had expected a more typical submission for a Bachelor of Business Administration program. They referred the University College's Bachelor of Technology plans to a special committee to examine the concept.[13] In May, D.F. Campbell was sent to meet the MPHEC to convince them to expedite the approval and implementation of UCCB programs and courses.[14] Positive results were spotty: the engineering and computer science degrees were approved in October, but the innovative Bachelor of Technology and Bachelor of Applied Management degrees were still being delayed—a year-and-a-half because the MPHEC was examining the "desirability" of offering such programs.[15] Approval for Applied Arts and Bachelor of Technology degrees was still being held up in the winter of 1984 since the MPHEC were "not sure how to handle such programs."[16]

Another pilgrimage was made to MPHEC in January 1984, this time by President Reid, to explain the aims and programs of the University College to them. He returned frustrated, since he was told all the innovative programs were categorized as ones the commission was not prepared to consider at the time.[17] The chairman of MPHEC's programs committee even suggested that UCCB proceed on programs without commission approval and apply political pressure to obtain course authorization. Reid got the message that this was the only way to overcome opposition to

UCCB's applications. There was "still some resistance to the existence of this institution."[18]

Frustrations continued. The University College long sought the Bachelor of Technology degree in Environmental Studies, which seemed very natural for an institution with a technology component situated in Cape Breton, where environmental concerns were becoming critical. While Reid went to the politicians for support, the Technical University of Nova Scotia (TUNS) in Halifax alleged the University College was transgressing into their territory. Reid responded that UCCB was seeking a technology—not an engineering—degree which indeed would have been within the purview of TUNS. The matter was left in the hands of the Nova Scotia cabinet.[19]

While this battle was taking place, UCCB's ten-year-long application effort to offer tourism and hospitality was lost to Mount St. Vincent University. Reid, who in effect had assumed most of the control of the University College's direction, felt a "great personal loss" in failing to obtain the program and told the MPHEC it was better adapted to UCCB than to a more traditional institution. The loss was even more galling since 150 applications for the program had been received.[20] Reid would have been even more frustrated could he have foreseen that the Bachelor of Science in Nursing, which was approved by College Council and submitted to the MPHEC during his time, would not receive even modified approval for 14 years.[21]

In contrast, programs where internal approval alone was needed moved along quickly. Especially notable were co-operative programs, whereby eight months of study was followed by alternate four-month periods of work and study. By 1988, the University College was offering nine technology programs in the co-operative format, in engineering, chemical, environmental, mechanical, mineral technology, and business technology programs with options in accounting, data processing, marketing management and paralegal technology.[22] In addition, in 1989, the innovative engineering technology program was the only one in Nova Scotia to receive full accreditation from the Canadian Council of Technicians and Technologists. Such innovative programs clearly reflected the aims and purpose of the institution.

The fortunes of Trades training were less positive. Changes in funding policies threatened the program, which in turn affected the tripartite nature of the University College, based as it was on the amalgamation of academic, technology, and trades disciplines. One factor in the decline of trades training was the growth of regional vocational schools, which drew off students from the University College. As well, in 1984 the provincial government instituted a policy making laid-off apprentices ineligible for training, which had a strong effect on Cape Breton where unemployment was high and layoffs were common.[23] The number of hours allotted by the provincial government to trades training at UCCB fell from 25,000 to 17,000 between 1984 and 1985, and to 10,000 in 1986.[24] Programs were peeled away one after another with enrolment dropping to just 12 people per course and with costs mounting to $1,200 per course. The University College even absorbed the full costs of two courses, auto body and industrial electrical, an expense of $30,000. Inevitably, the threat of instructor layoffs loomed. The 16 trades instructors put up a fight, alleging that plans were afoot to convert the University College into a liberal arts and technology institution only.[25] The administration claimed that more than sixty jobs were being cut in trades programs across the province and that changing skill needs were the cause.[26]

On this note, an internal task force recommended, in June 1986, the retraining of instructors in new skills. Though this was received positively and a trades instructor was engaged to work on ways of achieving additional allocations of training days, after meetings with provincial politicians, it was apparent that funding for institutional trades instruction would continue to decline—particularly as the private sector was undertaking more of its own training.[27] Between 1983 and 1986, Trades training had fallen from 12 to 3.5 percent of the university college budget,[28] a decline that continued for the rest of the decade. By October 1992, only 8-12 people were employed in Trades instruction, and though UCCB was willing to defend the program, a November forecast of a

$123,000 shortfall in tuition recovery from trades training in an already overburdened budget, held out gloomy prospects for the program.[29]

While Trades training witnessed declining numbers, the burgeoning increase in enrolment in other disciplines, together with increasing staff size, led to overcrowded conditions. By the early 1980s, faculty members had surpassed 100 with support staff at 120. Morale and tempers were affected as two or even three faculty were forced to share offices. As well, more students arriving from beyond the Sydney area favoured residential space on campus even though, in 1982, 350 homes were registered as willing to take in students.[30]

In 1980, plans had been made to set aside a capital fund of $1,000,000 for a two-house residence for 40 students.[31] It soon became evident however, that a 100-bed facility was needed.[32] For the next five years matters proceeded slowly, largely because it was decided a master plan for development was needed, involving not only residences and academic space, but a fund-raising strategy as well. Then attention was diverted to the Campus Centre expansion and buildings for hosting the Canada Winter Games planned for 1987. Finally, a building committee or task force was set up by the Board of Governors in October 1986 to invite proposals for a residence of 100 beds.[33] The committee could not find a local company interested in building a residence unless UCCB made a financial commitment.[34] This prodded the Board to reactivate capital fundraising plans of 1980, and they appointed a development committee early in January, 1987. It estimated a 100-bed residence would cost $2,500,000, with a total for all campus expansion of $13,000,000.[35]

The Development Committee took shape during 1987 and, finally, in October 1988 Joseph "Joe" Shannon, was appointed chair of the "Partners for Progress" financial campaign.[36] Shannon was a widely respected entrepreneur and developer. Under his leadership, a priority list of development needs for the campus was inaugurated, totalling close to $9,000,000, with the cost of the residence coming in at $2,000,000. The financial campaign, launched shortly after Shannon's appointment, was immediately successful. The provincial government committed

$4,600,000 to the cause.[37] Sixty percent of the faculty and staff contributed, as well as the Student Union. The extended Cape Breton community and alumni were involved in a Caper Festival, bringing in Cape Bretoners from all over the country.[38] By the end of 1988, six million dollars had been raised and the ten-million-dollar goal was within reach. Plans for a residence were drawn up when $500,000 was received from the J.W. McConnell Family Foundation.[39]

Various companies submitted plans with space for between 100 and 600 beds. Tenders were opened March 1, on a three-storey, 160-bed residence and the first sod was turned by Brian A. Young, Minister of Municipal Affairs, April 5, in the presence of staff, students and members of the public.[40] Costs rose to $2,800,000, which on a cost-per-bed estimate was far below that of other university residences in the region.[41] With furniture, total expenditures were $3,200,000.[42] The building was named "MacDonald Residence" in honour of the first donors to the college whose funds had been used over the years for many college projects, including the residence.[43] Premier Donald Cameron opened the building 15 September 1991 to a large crowd, including some demonstrating against low levels of funding for the university college. Although Cameron "appeared to be ill at ease with comments from the protesters," a gala dinner with 400 contributors to the "Partners for Progress" campaign was a sparkling success.[44]

An even more crucial need than the residence was academic and staff space. By 1985, space problems had become so serious that thought was being given to bringing back portable buildings, a throwback to the horror days in downtown Sydney.[45] Fear of this prodded the Board to look into adding extra floors to the library and Campus Centre, and a submission for this was placed before the MPHEC.[46] This would have added as many as eleven new classrooms, as well as seminar rooms, faculty offices, arts laboratories and student union space, at a cost of $3,000,000.[47] A task force was set up to deal with physical expansion plans.[48] While the plans for the residence had moved along, however, the campus centre expansion stalled. First of all, the MPHEC turned down participation in the expansion plans based on the mistaken assumption that the federal government was going to take up the project under the Cape Breton Advisory Committee, one of a myriad of bodies appointed to tackle the weakening Cape Breton economy.[49] Though this misunderstanding was soon cleared up, tight provincial government spending froze the plans again and the space problem worsened. In desperation, an appeal was made in 1988 to Edmund Morris, Minister of Education and Job Training, for space in the only partially occupied Adult Vocational Training Centre. This resulted in space there for offices, classrooms, and eventually some research facilities.[50] This coincided with the "Partners for Progress" campaign, which aspired to a four- to five-million-dollar expansion of the Campus Centre as part of its $10,000,000 fundraising project. Completed in September 1992, and after allocating $3,500,000 to the residence, approximately $6,000,000 was available for Campus Centre expansion.

More problems arose, however, when, in March 1991, Howard MacIntyre, Director of the Physical Plant, informed the board that new building codes would not allow the planned addition of new floors to the Campus Centre; any additions must take place horizontally.[51] This was alarming news when added to higher than estimated construction costs for the residence, effectively killing off hopes for expansion in the near term.

As it happened, a new expansionary project materialized in the form of the 1987 Canada Winter Games. The idea of attracting such an event to Cape Breton was first proposed by Donald Arseneau of the Bras d'Or Institute and was taken up in 1982 by D.F. Campbell, Allan Sullivan and Member of Parliament David Dingwall.[52] When, in 1984, Cape Breton was actually awarded the Games, a "Friends of the Games" fundraising campaign was organized. It was decided to locate a "Canada Games Complex" on the campus. The original plans called for a $9,600,000 free-standing structure featuring a 5,000 seat arena with an Olympic-sized rink, a sports institute, a sports medicine facility and classrooms.[53] The realities of funding and cost estimates took firmer hold during the next few years. The University College was expected to raise some of the funds, which it did with a $250,000 payment from the MacDonald Estate legacy, and the Friends of the Games promised $330,000 for equipment, but the University College had to agree to assume all legal obligations and financial risks relating to construction.[54] Board members were growing nervous, but they were assured that funding was firm—and besides, the opportunity was just too good to turn down.[55] Plans went ahead and fears were somewhat tempered by a scaling down of the original plans, which reduced proposed capacity to 3,500, but kept the sports institute and 10 classrooms at a cost of $4,000,000. Money was also to be saved by attaching the building to the existing Sullivan Field House.[56] Local architect, Robert Ojolick, himself a graduate of Xavier Junior College, finally came up with an impressive building seating 1,980 people—still one of the largest [university] ice arenas in eastern Canada.[57] The sod-turning took place 28 September 1985 and it was completed well in time for the February 1987 opening. The Games were a great success, the weather perfect. Cape Bretoners embraced the event as well as the new complex, which also was available for community use.

Still, money—the perennial factor—was a great worry. Cost-sharing discussions took place with the County of Cape Breton, the Friends of the Games and the Host Society. Happily, the games realized a surplus of $300,000. With money from the Friends of the Games ($200,000) and tax rebates, UCCB received an additional $700,000, which was put in scholarships ($150,000), a complex maintenance endowment ($150,000) and a Sports Heritage Centre.[58] Gifts worth $335,000 were also received for a sound system, scoreboards and extensive gymnasium equipment.[59] As well, the Max Bell Foundation announced it would donate up to $330,000 for a sports medicine clinic to go along with the complex. The Max Bell Sports Medicine Clinic, with the latest equipment was incorporated into the structure and became another permanent legacy of the Games.[60]

There were still concerns, however, with the cost of maintenance of the building. The Board had been assured by the Vice President Finance, Tom MacNeil, that the building would pay for itself, but questions about the costs of ice-making and staffing would not go away, despite the games endowment fund and the small profit the complex made in 1987-88. And it turned out that, despite rental fees from both the athletic department and the public, the complex began running deficits which would plague the increasingly cash-strapped institution during the 90s.[61]

Despite expanded facilities, growing enrolment, and an increasing number of programs, the basic administrative structure of the University College had not changed much since the union of the two campuses. As of 1979, it consisted of a Board of Governors with its committees to whom the president reported, and a College Council which dealt with academic questions. The Senior Vice-President of Administration, John Terry, had the responsibilities of program development including athletics, continuing education, campus improvement, the four institutes, and services like the computer office, the registrar, student services as well as the Information and Communications Centre, Reading and Writing Centre, the Library, and the Language Laboratory. Under the purview of the Academic Vice-President, William Gallivan, fell the Dean of Arts and Science, and Dean of Technology and Trades with their burgeoning programs, as well as research. Finally, the Treasurer/Comptroller Tom MacNeil, who, like the other two, reported directly to the president, managed financial services, budgets, purchasing and the physical plant.[62]

Long-standing jurisdictional disputes between the Arts and Science faculty and the Department of Continuing Education precipitated structural changes. The two areas fell under different vice-presidents, and many academics were still critical of the quality of innovative continuing education courses.[63] The Director of Continuing Education, Ora McManus, had presented a report in May 1981, drawing attention to the fact that the institution had a mandate to serve the community at all levels, and calling for even more community-based programs in his department, without which community support would be lost. As Continuing Education did not receive funding through the MPHEC, aggressive means had to be found to raise revenue by offering courses of community interest. One way of doing this was to offer part-time courses, many of which came under the jurisdiction of his department, even though duplicate courses were being offered by the Arts And Science faculty. In essence the institution was competing against itself. A study of the situation by the Board, released in February 1982 only caused more contention when it emphasized the innovative mandate of the institution and suggested that Continuing Education be made an equal partner with the two faculties—Arts and Science, and Trades and Technology.[64] The academic representatives on the Board refused to accept this and the report was circulated for comment throughout the institution. As a result, in June another committee recommended that Continuing Education come under the jurisdiction of the Academic Vice-President. After a spirited debate this new arrangement was adopted.[65]

The Board was stung by the vituperative arguments that had taken place as well as the revelations of administrative confusion, so a Structures Committee was appointed to examine the organization of the institution as a whole.[66] What followed was what President Reid called, "a great deal of upheaval and structural changes."[67] The Committee met and debated for a whole year and in February 1984 finally had a report. The office of Senior Vice-President Administration was eliminated to be replaced by a Vice-President Community Services. It was hoped that this would raise the profile of the University College in the community. Continuing Education and the institutes with their deep community roots, would fall under this jurisdiction headed by John Terry. The two other vice-presidents, Academic and Administration and Finance, under Gallivan and MacNeil, remained basically unchanged and still overburdened.[68]

Donald Fewer took over as the new Dean of Academic and Student Services reporting to the Academic Vice-President in order to focus on the needs of the growing student body.[69] He was replaced as registrar by Deanne Dennison, the first woman to hold a senior administrative post in the University College.[70] This, with the additional appointment of a Development Officer in 1988, remained the basic administrative structure for the remainder of Reid's term as president.[71]

Administrative re-organization could not, however, solve UCCB's growing financial problems. The 1980s began a trend of declining government support for universities. In the period 1980-1986 the ratio of government funding per $100 of tuition dropped from $5.50 to $3.50. Superficially, it would appear that funding kept pace. For example, in 1981-82, the university college received $6,227,000 from the provincial government; by 1989, due to rising enrolment, this had increased to $11,200,000. The truth, however, was that this was not enough to cover the costs of new programs, equipment needs, particularly in technology and science, and to meet the increasing role of the institution in the community. The shortfall had to be met by tuition increases which rose from $1,180 for arts and science and $750 for technology in 1986-87 to $1,780 and $1,165 respectively in 1988-89.[72] Enrolment, up by almost 100 percent 1983-93, by 25 percent in 1983-84 alone, brought in more money which helped, but did not eliminate, the gap between the provincial grant and the actual rising costs of delivering education.

The provincial grant to universities was based on a fixed funding formula that took into account the number of full-time and part-time students and the relative costs of different programs. UCCB received additional funding, but it still failed to adequately recognize the institution's special needs, particularly in technology, as well as the fact that it was growing far more quickly than the others. Moreover, expansion was occurring at a time when government funding was declining and the growth of the more established universities was slowing.[73] The additional amounts generally added only one-half to one percent to the base budget. This failed to satisfy the administration who claimed, in 1985 for example, that two to three percent or $400,000 would be a fairer amount.[74] Hence, though the university college had grown to become the sixth largest post-secondary institution in the Atlantic Region, its funding was the eighth.[75]

The result was a financial roller coaster whose ups and downs were greatly affected by the slightest change in student enrolment. For example, despite an enrolment increase of 15 percent in Arts And Science in 1983-84 alone, an operating deficit of $32,000 threatened to raise the accumulated deficit to $174,000.[76] Increased enrolment that year, however, led to increased income and an accumulated deficit of $141,452.[77] The same scenario held in 1984, reducing the accumulated deficit to $41,953.[78]

Though Reid prided the University College on its control over spending, it was achieved mainly by tuition hikes (which rose 12 percent in that year alone), and neglect of the physical plant. Reid, MacNeil, and Gallivan engaged in the frustrating exercise of trying to convince the government and its agencies of the need for additional funding based on the institution's special program expansion costs. They convinced the MPHEC to come across with a recommendation for an extra $518,000 for 1985-86, with a further $1,200,000, and $1,800,000 over base funding for the following two years. This would mean that UCCB's grant would be at a par with other universities and the funding formula could henceforth be applied without the highly unreliable extra grants it had to depend upon to survive each year.[79] Their hopes were dashed when instead of $518,000 for the first year, only $160,000 was received.[80] Reid, always the optimist, continued to look forward to a new funding formula that would put UCCB on the same financial footing as the other universities, but this was not forthcoming. Faced with another five-percent tuition hike, Gallivan suggested that individual course costs be frozen at 1985 levels; but increasing costs could not be avoided and tuition increases were approved.[81] The result was a surplus which Reid declared wiped out the deficit.[82] A further tuition increase of six percent in 1986-87 even allowed hiring of one new staff member each in French, English, Speech Communication, and Hospitality Administration, together with three new hires in the Registrar's office.[83]

In 1987, the roller coaster plunged again. The provincial government announced only a 4.1 percent increase in enrolment grants, meaning UCCB would be receiving only two-thirds of the full formula funding. Worse still, program development costs, salary settlements, a projected decline in enrolment and emergency building renovations threatened a deficit of $638,000.[84] Everything had to be quickly tightened. Department budgets were ordered cut by 10 percent and strict regulation of non-budgeted expenditures was inaugurated. Even more drastically, the Board was forced to take $200,000 from the $390,000 MacDonald Estate fund to reduce the deficit. It was deemed that it was legally proper to use the fund for building renovations since a large part of the deficit was a result of renovation costs.[85] Though MacNeil and Reid assured the board that the resultant deficit was only 2.5 percent worse than the amount budgeted, and that all universities were suffering from inadequate funding, the board demanded regular updates on expenditures, with board approval for expenditures over $50,000.

The next year looked even more frightening. Gallivan told the executive of the board that UCCB might expect an increase of only 2.4 percent in its grant, its lowest percentage increase ever, and the second lowest dollar increase in the province. Quick telephone calls and meetings managed to raise the increase to 4.73 percent over 1987.[86] Belt tightening and yet another tuition increase of 4 percent in 1988 saw the situation improve.[87] The University College came in below budget while revenues exceeded expenditures by $308,000. This brought the $410,000 deficit of 1987 to $130,000 in 1988.[88] That April, before another crisis could erupt, the Board managed to get the Minister of Higher Education, Edmund Morris, to come to Sydney to see the situation for himself. He was treated to a full explanation of the problems. This included the extra cost of technology programs which other universities did not face, as well as the special community education programs like the widely-acclaimed Co-op Placement program which cost the institution $250,000 per year, and which received no provincial funding. Though Morris would not commit to any special consideration for the University College beyond the extra, stop-gap funding UCCB usually received ($255,000 that year), he did seem to recognize the complexity of the young institution's problems by suggesting that a committee—composed of the chairman of the Board, Dr. Kenneth MacLennan, President Reid, members of the community and himself—be organized to gain a "long-horizons look." The "Horizons Commission," which promised to be the first such university committee ever set up in Nova Scotia, was to come up with non-binding recommendations for a long-term development strategy for UCCB, including its relationship with the Nova Scotia Community College system.[89]

The promise of finally getting the province to take the situation seriously was dashed when Edmund Morris resigned from Cabinet. This was followed by a provincial election and the hopes pinned on the Horizons Commission vanished.[90] UCCB did, however, appoint an internal Horizons Committee and began adding to the changes it wanted to see implemented. Besides financial questions, the University College wanted its equality with older universities recognized by amending its charter to allow the appointment of a chancellor, to finally eliminate St. Francis Xavier University appointments to the Board and to dispense with the unwarranted provision for governmental approval of new programs. As well, UCCB was the only university with direct government appointees on its board; other universities simply submitted a list of names for governmental approval.[91]

Joel Matheson, the new Minister of Advanced Education and Job Training in the Buchanan government, advised administration "to slow down, for a short while with respect to its own Horizons Committee's activities." The provincial government had appointed a committee under the chairmanship of A.K. Addlington to examine the university and community college funding formula. Addlington recommended that the enrolment-driven, equity-based funding formula be dropped and that each university come up with a "planned capacity and role" statement, that is, a self-analysis of its institutional operations, showing how they fit into the overall university system and how the university planned to attain these goals. Enrolment would decline in importance as part of basic funding. Instead, incentives would be given toward helping institutions attain goals of quality rather than mere size of programs, and rewards would be given to certain objectives, such as technology transfer to Canadian industry.[92]

Since the government accepted the report, much of 1989 was taken up with drawing up a Role and Capacity Statement for the minister and the MPHEC. This entailed a study of each department for the ensuing five years, for projected enrolment, capital and staffing requirements.[93]

Meanwhile, the University College's financial situation continued to darken. The 1989 increase in the government grant was 3.9 percent, the lowest percentage for all universities in Nova Scotia; in the wake of the Addlington recommendations, very little money had been earmarked for new programs, and college council became alarmed at the impact of a threatened large deficit on these programs.[94] The immediate response was a proposed budget with a tuition increase of 6.6 percent in Arts and Science, 9.4 percent in Technology and Trades and 5.7 percent for part-time studies. As well, a discontinuation of certain programs was under consideration. This still would not reduce the deficit threatening to balloon to more than $600,000 in the coming year. Discussion as to whether and how the deficit should be eliminated was acrimonious. College Council resisted cutbacks, which would emasculate programs, and some encouraged the concept of a deficit at $600,000 "plus." It was agreed programs should be saved and the budget was adopted.[95]

The tuition increase brought in more revenue, while decreased expenditures eventually led to a projected deficit for 1989-90 at around $321,881.[96] Still however, any unexpected expense could lead to a more serious financial situation and no one had a clear view of an immediate solution to the problem of balancing programs and finances.

The last days of William Reid's presidency were in many ways a disappointment to him. He had been intimately involved with the development of the University College since its early days. As president, he had largely assumed control of operations and problems rested heavily on his shoulders. Yet, as a life-long local academic, he had little influence on government funders; the fiscal operations of the institution were being questioned, though he had only slight control over its financial direction.[97] In all his years at the institution he could only remember an uphill battle. "We are the champion underdog," he explained at his last Board meeting, and he hoped the Board "would continue that fight until we have what every other population base has in this country of ours."[98]

The discontent bothering Reid was felt by the Board as well, but for somewhat different reasons. Chairman Dr. Kenneth MacLennan, suggested that he and other board members felt left out of the decision-making process and that matters on its agenda had already been decided by senior administration; their approval was only formality. He felt he did not know what was happening at the University College.[99] Just a month before Tom MacNeil had brought the news of a possible serious deficit, MacLellan had expressed his opinion that UCCB was in a "reasonably good financial state."[100] Reid, on the other hand, thought the board was trying to pry into administrative matters which "emasculated" senior administration and created disharmony. His feeling was that the Board should support the administration more strongly. "If the UCCB President is deemed to be a puppet, the office will not attract people of appropriate academic stature," he declared.[101] Like academic members of the Board, he also felt that individual members failed to use their influence to promote the claims of the University College with government power-brokers. As an academic, Reid himself had few influential connections and it seems little respect in the Halifax seats of power.[102]

MacLennan however, was worried that in its head-long rush to develop new programs, the University College had neglected broad policies directing the institution. He wondered about the lack of long-range planning, program evaluations, collective agreements, strategies for dealing with governments and management training.[103] He also worried about the perception of UCCB within the local community. Many people in Sydney regretted the University College's location, far from the downtown core, in an "ivory tower," drifting away from its role as a community resource. When the Academic Vice-President, Bill Gallivan, criticized the community's reaction to its economic problems, MacLennan was in turn highly critical of his attitude. Gregory MacLeod, a faculty member with his finger on the pulse of the community, openly proclaimed that "there's a lot of dissatisfaction within faculty about the approach taken by the Board and senior administration to the community." [104]

Reid left the presidency June 30, 1989. He had valiantly tried to achieve the long-held vision of a community-oriented university with innovative programs reflecting that concept. He had become frustrated by internal division over programs, deficits, harmful government policies, and community relations. The overwhelming growth of the institution, plagued by inadequate funding, presented a crushing challenge and minor administrative changes and financial tinkering would not avert the looming crisis.

VI

Pressures and Fissures, 1989-1992

The search for a new president to meet these threats took place during the fall and winter of 1989-90. By December the field had been narrowed to eight and by February, Board Chair, Dr. Kenneth MacLennan, announced that Dr. Peter Hill had agreed to a six-year contract beginning July 1, 1989. Forty-four years old and father of three, Hill was a native of Kentville, Nova Scotia, who had spent seven years as principal of the Sutherland Campus of Sir Sandford Flemming College in Peterborough, Ontario. As such, he knew the problems of a small institution: "I am extremely enthusiastic about the university. I know the challenges will come to me and I won't have to seek them out."[1]

Hill had studied examples of university colleges in Sweden and felt the model could work in Cape Breton. This would involve putting in place an integrated curriculum, with technology students taking core humanities courses, while academic pupils became competent in at least one field of technology. He knew that it would be difficult to be the first Canadian institution of higher learning to attempt this; it would be easier to be ranked with other, standard institutions, but this was not his vision. He thought a new model could be obtained only by quick action, integrating the faculty and at the same time emphasizing student centredness in an enjoyable atmosphere which would draw students to the University College.[2]

Enthusiasm was one of the brightest qualities Hill brought to the position. His winning personality and casual friendliness with staff and students made him immediately popular. He adopted the practice of meeting students in the hallways and eating in the open cafeteria; students and faculty addressed him on a first-name basis. It appeared that relations between administration and faculty and students might improve and the rapid-fire changes soon began.

By the Fall, Hill called for board approval to proceed with plans for a new residence and an expansion of the Campus Centre.[3] For the first time an open twelve-member Budget Committee was established to organize budget priorities and procedures, operational and capital; to review departmental budgets; and to review administrative decisions through regular reporting to ensure they were consistent with established priorities and practice.[4] Previously, departments and sub-departments had simply submitted budgets to senior administration by adding percentage increases to line items. Priorities and reviews were unknown at all but the most senior levels.

The new openness kept Hill on a popular footing. Guaranteed to bring him further approval was his organization of a Professional Development Committee to establish mechanisms for faculty travel, and the integration of professional development with sabbatical and other leaves. Sabbaticals, always in short supply, were jealously sought and criticized by winners and losers alike. A rational process was welcome.[5] Even more dramatically, in less than six months after his appointment, Hill proposed a new administrative structure, which was approved by the Board with the hope it would save money. The structure of the organization was flatter than the previously pyramidal one, with more people reporting directly to each senior administrator and more delegated decision-making. Representational consultative committees, such as budget, space, staff development, and planning and priorities, were organized to advise the president and the Board. More drastically, in an attempt to force the integration of the academic and technology faculties, the previous teaching divisions were broken down into schools which crossed disciplinary lines. Hence, deans of Applied Science and Technology, Arts and Social Science, Development Studies and Applied Arts, and Business, were appointed to head the schools. In an attempt to integrate continuing education into the fabric of the University College, and to end the long debate as to the status of extension, a Dean of Extension and Community Affairs was also appointed.[6]

Much-needed new departments were inaugurated in order to meet the demands of the growing institution. Major departmental innovations included: Research and Development which encompassed the long-established institutes and whose executive-director was in senior management, Alumni and Development, Computer Services, Marketing, Purchasing, Human Resources, Student Services, and Co-op Placements.[7] The position of Chief Librarian was raised to that of a senior administrator, reporting to the president, while former senior administrative positions remained in place.[8] Besides the president, Tom MacNeil, Executive Vice-President Administration and Finance, and Bill Gallivan, Vice President Academic, retained their positions. Hill hoped that a flatter organization would, by delegating authority, shorten the decision-making process and, with single points of contact, give greater flexibility in responding to the community. It also brought Hill into more direct contact with department heads, giving him greater control over the administration, so that all changes, whether successful or not, were credited to him.[9]

If the faculty and community wanted change, they got it. In keeping with his personality Hill explained he had acted quickly to minimize the distress that change always brings. In most cases, after consulting with the vice-presidents, he had asked individuals to fill the positions, old and new. The new organization was seen as a pilot project until July 1, 1991, at which time incumbents would be hired through normal processes.[10] In many cases, where people did not later resign, incumbents had simply stayed on for many years, with no further formalization of their position.[11]

Hill met with union presidents and faculty chairmen, and then with the whole faculty, before releasing his plans. This was followed by regular monthly meetings with faculty, a process which smoothed acceptance of the changes. These meetings were supplemented with popular casual sessions with faculty and staff, featuring snacks and refreshments. Hill's winning ways, enthusiasm and openness went a long way in gaining acceptance for the relatively revolutionary changes that endured well beyond his term in office.

All the administrative changes in the world, however, could not eliminate the financial problems that continued to plague the institution. Hill feared a projected deficit in 1989 of $660,000 and tried to get Joel Matheson, the Minister of Advanced Education and Job Training, to equalize the overhead grants of College (technology) and University students, which alone would increase the operating grant by over $2,000,000. He wanted to charge College students the same tuition as University students in order to net another $1,700,000.[12]

Trying to free UCCB from complete financial dependence on the provincial government, Hill also approached the Enterprise Cape Breton Corporation (ECBC), a Crown Corporation which had evolved from the Industrial Development Division of the Cape Breton Development Corporation (DEVCO). Its purpose was to broaden the economic base of Cape Breton Island, and its president, Pat Bates, himself a Cape Bretoner, realized the importance of the University College in developing high technology as a possible means of accomplishing this. During the winter of 1990 work was underway to develop a Memorandum of Understanding between the two agencies, whereby ECBC would supply funding for practical high-tech research to be carried out at UCCB. By March, ECBC agreed to grant $200,000 for the organization of an Environmental Services Laboratory at UCCB to perform research on the pollution-filled Sydney Tar Ponds.[13] This was the first of many activities which soon included scientific, cultural and tourism projects, that eventually brought over $5,000,000 in funding and developed the university college's research capacity as well as its role in community economic development.

The partnership was in keeping with Hill's vision of the University College. His installation on April 5, 1990 was a gala affair with representatives from 18 universities and colleges from 6 different provinces present. Hill was sworn in by Board chairman, Irving Schwartz, a popular local entrepreneur. Hill proclaimed the University College as a "catalyst for change and economic growth in Cape Breton," and as a centre for research and development. He was in tune with the latest thinking, explaining that universities had to work with government, business and the community by forming "partnerships."[14] He had already moved in this direction by twinning the University College with Western Community College in Newfoundland, thereby increasing enrolment from there to 26 out of 61 students from outside Nova Scotia. As well, the number of students from New Brunswick rose from one to nineteen.[15]

Hill's rapid changes rekindled the old problem of the relationship between the Board and the Administration. Joseph (Joe) Shannon, former chair of the "Partners for Progress" fund raiser, a Board member and self-made wealthy local entrepreneur with no university background, wanted the relationship between the Board and administration clarified to avoid areas of "improper infringement."[16] The Chairman of the Board, Irving Schwartz, and member lawyer George Unsworth asked administration to establish a Strategic Planning Process by the fall of 1990 to examine all segments of the University College, including the roles of the various elements and its overall mission.[17]

In the meantime, events moved quickly. Hill's new budgetary process began to kick in with each department setting priorities while the Board was to decide what could and could not be done. Hill hoped this would demonstrate to them their role in the administrative process.[18] The budgetary process itself was compromised by further cuts of transfer money from the federal to the provincial government. Hill worried that the University College's grant would increase by only four percent ($450,000), which a planned rise in salaries (of seven percent) would easily absorb. He could only hope for a favourable interpretation of the institution's Role and Capacity statement or an increase in CAD/CAM revenues which might bring in more money.[19]

The Budget Committee met all that Spring seeking ways of generating new revenues, or shifting money from non-academic to academic areas, and moving money to growth areas. A plan was developed to raise full-time tuition from $1,780 for University and $1,165 for College students in 1989 to $2,250 each by 1994-94, based on the assumption that College students should eventually pay the same fees as University students since they enjoyed the same services. This was considered the only way to make up for the provincial government's refusal to subsidize College and University tuitions to the same levels.[20] The board still felt the increases were too steep, but Hill convinced them that tuition rates had little influence on where students studied. Indeed, reports were already out that though tuitions were going to rise in 1990-91, applications were up by 25 percent over the previous year. [21]

Hill's victory was short-lived. Though he claimed there was a $30,000 surplus on the books when he arrived, during the spring of 1990, Tom MacNeil reported a deficit of between $300,000 and 600,000.[22] The Budget Committee, acting on the advice of the Planning and Priorities Committee, decided to save money by practically eliminating capital spending. Money thus saved would be spent on new hires and up to 20 sabbaticals. Shannon in particular was concerned over these plans, believing that maybe too much emphasis had been placed on quick faculty and staff growth. He also thought it unrealistic to pass a budget, balanced or not, with no capital expenditures. Consequently, the Board rejected the proposed budget and sent it back for revisions.[23]

The conflict over the budget was only one of a number of contentious issues between Hill and the Board. Just after his appointment, in an apparent move to raise the University College to a larger playing field, so to speak, Hill decided to organize a varsity football team. Hill hired J.I. Albrecht, former general manager of the Montreal Alouettes and very well-connected in the world of professional sports, as new athletics director, replacing Carl "Bucky" Buchanan (who had misgivings about Albrecht's abilities).[24] Albrecht's ambitious plan was to fully integrate UCCB's athletics program into the Atlantic Universities Athletic Association (AUAA).[25] Under Buchanan, UCCB had moved from the Nova Scotia Athletics Association, entered the AUAA in four sports programs: hockey, men's and women's soccer and women's basketball. Football, however, was a much more dramatic and expensive proposition and Buchanan had felt it was too early for the institution to enter that sport.[26] Faced with a tightening budget, Hill decided to raise external funds with a Hall of Fame hockey game. In raising money for football, he upset Shannon, who worried that it might draw attention from the University College's major financial campaign.[27] The event reportedly raised $100,000 with over 4,700 in attendance.[28]

Shannon was suspicious of the money figure, however, and he became more critical of other moves by Hill.[29] The latter had decided to renovate an area near the art gallery as a much-desired faculty and student lounge, even though, like football, no money had been budgeted for this. Though the move was popular with staff and students, the Board was highly critical of such expenditures in light of the growing deficit. With the local economy in decline and interest rates climbing, Shannon declared that expenditures must be curtailed. Yet it seemed that the following year's deficit would be even higher. He and Hill were accordingly at odds over priorities and jurisdiction: they could not even agree that these matters should be discussed by the Board's executive. Schwartz struggled to bring the two together, but the breach was widening.[30]

In ongoing discussions Hill tried to pare the budget, predicting a "possible" operating surplus of $133,000, though this still did not include provisions for capital expenditures. He compromised however, in deferring new hires and some sabbatical replacements.[31] By this he hoped to find $200,000 for capital, but Shannon, Schwartz, and Board member John Strasser, Vice-President of Sydney Steel, who also insisted on close budgetary control, made sure that they were on a Capital Allocations Committee along with Hill, Bill Gallivan, and Tom MacNeil.[32]

At this point, Shannon and Strasser's distrust of Hill and indeed of senior administration, was almost palpable. Shannon complained that the Board was continually being placed in a re-active position; that there always seemed to be a crisis, whether it be the "sudden" need for 18 new hires, the commitment of $200,000 for sabbaticals, or the unforeseen need for thousands of dollars to operate the Hill-spawned, unbudgeted Environmental Services Laboratory. He was nonplussed by academic life where people were always "coming and going." To the cautious businessman, university affairs appeared chaotic. Though he finally agreed to the hiring of three new people, matters were at the breaking point.[33] The Board refused to undertake further hires and any major capital expenditures.

The operations of the University College had now passed into the hands of the Board, and Hill was clearly outside the decision-making process. All he could do was point out that the province had made "targeted funding" money available to develop certain programs, such as Mi'kmaq Studies, the Novanet interactive computer program for the library, or the indirect costs of some programs in science and mathematics.[34] However, this did not penetrate to the root of the problem, which was the Board's lack of confidence in Hill's ability to handle the budget. Hill on the other hand, met privately with Schwartz and came away happy, believing that the complementary but distinct roles of the Board and the administration had been cleared up. Still, as an academic, he remained adamant as to his right to grant sabbatical leaves even with finances as tight as they were.[35]

Hill's final attempt at saving his budget and his very job occurred at the end of June. He proposed to the Board that $100,000 be allocated for retirement of the deficit, and that capital spending be limited to $60,000 unless further funds materialized. His resolution was defeated. Strasser then moved that no new money be allocated for deficit retirement, that the deficit be retired beginning in 1991-92, and that $400,000 be set aside for capital expenditures. This was carried. Even though Hill seconded Strasser's motion, his fate was sealed. All his plans as chief administrator had been rejected.[36]

It was at this meeting that Schwartz noted that, after one year in office, Hill's contract was up for review by questionnaire to administrative staff, department heads, and students.[37] It also included a self-evaluation by Hill, comparing his objectives and accomplishments. The Board's Executive Committee, with the exception of members employed by UCCB, were also to carry out the review, to be completed within 30 days.

Hill was exhausted. Despite warnings that his job was in jeopardy, he decided to leave for a European conference during the review and was absent for its subsequent executive meeting, held off-campus at Sydney Steel.[38] During the month of July, plans were being made to replace Hill on an interim basis with John Terry who agreed not to be a candidate for the presidency. Terry was an obvious choice because of his long association with NSEIT and the University College. As well, he had been dropped from senior administration in Hill's reorganization of the institution and most of his former duties had been subsumed by the Research and Development office.[39] Terry headed up a management group made up of himself, the Academic Vice-President, Bill Gallivan, and five Board members: Joe Shannon, Willie Sneddon, John Strasser, George Unsworth, and Gregory O'Keefe.[40] In effect, the institution was being run by the Executive of the Board of Governors.

Schwartz met Hill on August 13, presented him with a summary of the findings of the review committee, and told him that the Board Executive that day had decided to terminate his contract. A list of reasons was presented, including Hill's having placed the financial viability of the university college in jeopardy and his disregard for the collegial process. Hill, in response, requested to be allowed to speak to the Board the following day for half an hour. The following day the Board did meet but it refused Hill's request. A formal motion was then passed by the Board terminating Hill's contract[41] and a Search Committee was immediately organized to find his replacement.[42]

What Schwartz referred to as a "very sad day" in the aftermath of the firing, was only the prelude to two-and-a-half year period of calamity and tension, which weighed heavily on the whole institution. Hill left, saying, "I think the Board's decision was inappropriate and there was no criteria for making such a decision," adding that he believed his contract had been broken.[43] Hill allegedly made other comments against Shannon and the board, which he was apparently willing to stand by—comments that elicited notice of legal action against him.[44]

For the following week, an open battle was waged in the press, shocking not only the Island but the rest of the country as well. Hill pointed out a problem that had existed long before his tenure:

> There is a misunderstanding by some of the board as to its exact role. The role of the board is not to run the institution; that is the role of the president, administration and faculty.[45]

He went on to claim that the decision to fire him was a "conspiracy" by those opposed to the changes he had made, which he felt were important not only for the University College, but for the whole of Cape Breton, "but change here tends to be the exception rather than the norm."[46] He added, "The community is ready for that type of change, but there is a ruling class that doesn't see themselves as benefiting from change."[47] He absolved himself from causing the deficit, which he blamed on the University College's failure to enact proper policies and procedures governing purchasing and spending. He felt there had been unpaid bills which had been kept off the books, which gave the false appearance of a balanced budget.[48] As he prepared to vacate his office, he commented: "I think I made a difference and some of those differences will stick."[49]

More seriously, the press quoted Hill as saying that Shannon was in a conflict of interest because some of his companies might well bid on construction contracts at the University College. The public knew that Shannon was chairman of the "Partners for Progress" drive to raise funds for the institution's expansion, and this allegation deeply upset him, particularly since he had taken moves to separate himself from the tendering committee. The Board had even passed a resolution that no conflict of interest existed in his case.[50]

Meanwhile, the faculty had entered the fray, condemning the board for acting without consultation, and especially its appointment of a Management Committee charged with running the institution:

> Such a new and unwarranted committee is assuming the responsibilities that properly rest with the president, administration and the faculty and staff in accordance with long standing University College traditions and procedures.[51]

These confrontations left the students in a dilemma. Though still on summer break, the confusion as to the role of the Board, the administration and faculty baffled them. Their president, Bob MacLean, though a member of the board which had unanimously voted to oust Hill, refused to take a position in the struggle.[52] Hill had been popular with the students, initiating an "open-door policy," and supporting the football team.[53]

By this time, rumours were growing as quickly as morale was sinking. John Terry and Irving Schwartz called a general assembly in the Playhouse to explain the situation. Schwartz reiterated that Hill had committed the university college to projects and had made program decisions without input from either the board or administration and underlined this by drawing attention to UCCB's ever-growing deficit—now $580,000. In the hope of showing the institution's stability, John Terry announced that Hill's re-organization plans would continue and appointments would remain, to be reviewed in accordance with recognized procedures.[54]

The drama was heightened when Hill himself finally addressed the assembly. To a round of applause, he took the stage to reiterate his feeling that the university college must govern itself, the only true question being what people wanted the school to be.[55] After the meeting both sides repeated their plans to go to court, Hill to obtain reinstatement, the Board to protect the reputation of Board members, represented in this case by Joe Shannon.[56] Despite the contention, Schwartz was happy with the meeting and felt that most members of the University College agreed with the firing. He was probably even happier that his term as Chairman of the Board had only a little over a month to run, but he was far from finished.[57] A community-based group, concerned about the future of the institution, "the Alumni and Friends of UCCB," was formed in mid-October and called a meeting at the Steel Workers Hall in Sydney. Hill addressed the crowd of about 50 people and agreed with the Board's position that there was a difference in management style between them. Some faculty members and at least one board member were present, but few students took part. Hill closed his address calling for the support of student, faculty, and the press in his attempt to regain his post.[58] Though Alumni And Friends tried to raise community involvement, the Board ignored its request to send a representative to address their meeting.[59]

With the new term in full swing, further stresses erupted. In November, a brawl broke out at a UCCB dance, resulting in one student's being badly hurt and three people being taken to hospital. The RCMP claimed that UCCB dances were becoming the scene of frequent fights.[60] Then there was the football team, organized in the spring of 1990, with recruitment of many players from off-island. The first game in September, played at the Coast Guard College (where the uprights were set in concrete just one day before), resulted in a resounding victory for UCCB, a much-needed morale booster. The university college seemed to be proving it could compete and win against the more established universities, but at what cost? Original budget estimates for varsity football of $135,000, which it was hoped would be recovered outside the regular budget through sponsorships, had by August already spiralled to well over $200,000 and it was hinted that the cost of some items had been buried "elsewhere."[61] Despite this, it was decided to press on with the program, and the first game victory and further excellent performances by the team delighted students and faculty. Large crowds, with Peter Hill in attendance, brought much of the university college together during a time of growing division.

After the season ended, however, problems emerged which put Hill and his senior administrators in a bad light. It was revealed that some of the players had received free tuition for 1990-91 as well as subsidized accommodations, and that costs had spiralled well beyond estimates. Transportation and meals for players, which it had been estimated in June would cost $18,000, by October alone amounted to $35,000. By the same month, though there had been no provision for them in the budget, telephone calls made by some players to their homes in Britain or the United States cost $7,327.[62] Therefore, the Executive of the Board refused to make a commitment to football for the next season despite the fact that students began a drive to save it. The campaign attracted national media coverage, and students collected a 2,400-name petition in support of the program. Even though some Board members still supported the cause, no commitment was made.[63] As is often the case with other universities, the high cost of football outweighed the potentially unifying school spirit it may have fostered.

The issue was soon subsumed by the overall budget crisis that broke that fall (1990). Stern measures would have to be taken to curb spending, and when in October the board chose the unrelenting Joe Shannon as Board Chair to replace Irving Schwartz, who had been tireless in his attempts to quell tensions, there was little doubt such tensions would erupt.[64] Shannon had been critical of Hill's spending and had been actively involved in his dismissal. He was now ready to turn his attention to the Finance Department of the University College. At Shannon's first meeting of the Board Executive, Tom MacNeil was able to report that as of late September, expenditures were slightly under budget with bank indebtedness at $831,004. Accounts receivable amounted to $764,371 and tuition payments were still coming in.[65]

By the end of November however, more alarming figures were presented by the Board's auditing committee. The institution's overall deficit which had been $1,082,983 in September was now $1,824,162.[66] MacNeil reported that expected revenues had failed to materialize and held little hope for new sources. Bills for the new lounge ($218,000) and football team ($130,000) continued to roll in. Athletics costs, which had been $408,000 in 1989-90, had grown to $610,000 in 1990-91. The cost of Hill's academic restructuring was more than $375,000, followed by new hires ($364,000) and sabbatical replacements ($214,000). [67]

With no clear system of spending authorities in place, matters looked grim. Board members called for an "honest budget" for the following year, and John Terry promised this would be the case.[68] The first problem was the interpretation of the figures. Operating and capital accounts had not been clearly separated, including certain capital expenditures on the lounge and the football program. MacNeil began the process of clearing this up and outlining costs due to the amortization of earlier items, such as a new main computer and phone system.[69]

The pressure to control the deficit was all the more urgent since the MPHEC had ruled that if a university's annual deficit rose above two percent of its annual operating grant, this amount must be clawed back by a reduction of two percent of the following year's operating grant. If this were not done, the MPHEC could suspend any new programs and capital projects.[70] The budgetary process which began in January 1991 threatened to be the most difficult in the history of the University College. Each budget manager began working on ideal budgets which were gradually reduced to show the effects such a loss would have on the department. Capital costs were to be clearly separated out and listed in order of priority and the full budgetary committee, now including deans, administrators and section heads would decide on spending priorities.[71]

Regular meetings of the budget committee became painful. Probing questions from a now-cynical staff were aimed at MacNeil, but what was perceived as his "inability and/or unwillingness to provide the Budget Committee with information it considered essential in its deliberations," slowed the process.[72] Then suddenly, at the end of January, an anonymous document entitled "How Expensive is Football?" was brought to the attention of the board. Tom MacNeil, to whom the Athletic Department reported, had brought it to John Terry's attention in mid-December, but because it was anonymous, Terry had dismissed it. However, rumours as to the existence of the letter and its contents swirled around the campus and beyond, leading Board members to seek an investigation of the allegations, centred as they were on the effects of the costs of football on the current budget.[73] Though the contents were kept secret, John Terry later made statements indicating that the document alleged that Athletic Director Albrecht and MacNeil had attended a Vanier Cup game in Toronto at the expense of the University College and that free board and lodging, as well as tuition wavers, had been given football players, in violation of university football regulations.[74] Whatever the truth of the letter, MacNeil was angered that an anonymous document was even being discussed by the board, refused to answer questions and walked out of the meeting.[75]

Terry met with MacNeil and, persuaded that MacNeil's behaviour was due to mounting pressures, convinced him to take a month's vacation in February.[76] Keith Sanderson, of the Department of Management and Administration, agreed to undertake the pecuniary responsibilities of Director of Administration and Finance and provide information necessary for the budget committee's deliberations.[77]

Budgetary deliberations during February proceeded on a more peaceful note. Immediate "discretionary" cuts of $100,000 were made across the institution, including library book ordering and travel, in order to stem the outflow of money.[78] Needless to say, the Budget Committee was quick to take vengeance on what it perceived to be the expenditures wasted on football. It placed athletics very low on its list of spending priorities and recommended the cancellation of football. On the same day, the Executive of the Board unanimously recommended the elimination of the football program.[79] The full Board accepted the recommendation the next day despite a noisy demonstration of students outside the boardroom supporting the program.[80] The cancellation came just days after it was learned that the University College was under investigation by the Canadian Interuniversity Athletic Union over allegations it had given too much financial assistance to student athletes. The local press drew attention to the fact that allegations were being made that the institution had paid air fares for some football players to fly home for Christmas break and to house some players at a local hotel. Terry reported that as shocking as this was, the investigation was actually over a member of the hockey team.[81]

Despite disruptions and pressure, the 29-member Budget Committee came up with a budget on 1 March. It was approved by the Board with revenues of $19,596,395 ($18,586,501 in 1991), expenditures of $19,496,395 ($18,737,589 in 1991), with a deficit reduction of $100,000.[82] Money was set aside for the hiring of a comptroller, and plans were made to study policies of mandatory retirement and deficit reduction.[83]

The day before the budget was to be approved, however, John Terry revealed to the Executive of the Board that the Auditor General of Nova Scotia had advised him that the University College should undertake a complete review of its entire financial management process. A long list of subjects were to be tackled, such as an investigation of all policies of the Vice President Administration and Finance's Department, financial responsibilities of Board members, accounting and purchasing policies, accountability of the Extension Department's non-credit course offerings, as well as capital expenditures to ensure that they were in line with MPHEC guidelines. Expenditures of the bookstore, the CAD/CAM centre, the Environmental Services Lab, and the Canada Games Complex, which were not included in the 1991-92 budget, were to be included. If these departments' budgets had been included in the 1991-92 budget they would have added over $1,400,000 to the bottom line.[84]

Such open questioning of financial operations was bound to reflect poorly on Tom MacNeil's stewardship. Yet in all the years he had been in charge of the institution's finances, his figures and procedures had rarely been questioned. Indeed, he had been praised by successive boards for his work in guiding its finances and, as calls grew for his dismissal, John Terry, naively perhaps, stood by him.[85] He could find no documented evidence to support the dismissal and felt it was unfair to blame MacNeil for all of UCCB's financial woes. He did however meet with MacNeil and flatly told him that his personal attitude toward his subordinates needed improvement and his return from leave was probationary, dependent upon his performance. In addition, he had to relinquish control over athletics and the physical plant. Despite these restraints, all but one dean, the Academic Vice-President and faculty representative on the Executive of the Board opposed reinstatement. Terry persisted, however, and the Executive agreed that MacNeil should discuss matters with his staff and keep a low profile during the ensuing weeks of his return.[86]

It was not only senior administration that opposed MacNeil's return. Students, faculty and the community joined in the fray. John Terry, despite extreme emotional pressure at times apparently near the breaking point, stood firm. With Shannon, he went before a "raucous" meeting with 250 students, which was termed an "accountability session." Students grilled Terry and Shannon on Hill's firing, athletics, and of course the MacNeil situation. Terry reiterated that there was nothing to suggest that the financial problems of the university college were the result of the actions of MacNeil or his staff. Little changed, however, as a result of the meeting. As Student Union president Bob MacLean, said: "Morale is on a general decline and that includes everyone directly involved with the University."[87]

This included many of the faculty of Arts And Science who met a week later and passed, by a vote of 26 to 24, a non-confidence motion in John Terry. Terry remained firm, stating: "I am not going to be stampeded by elements inside or outside of this university to leave my job."[88] The Faculty of Trades and Technology supported their former boss, however, and passed a motion of confidence in him.[89] The "elements outside" the University were mainly the Alumni and Friends of UCCB group, who raised numerous questions as to the inside operations of the University College.[90]

The swirl of conflict abated somewhat in April. MacNeil was quietly back and Elizabeth Cooper had been hired for the position of comptroller. Though she reported to MacNeil, the fact that she had no earlier connections to the institution and was an outstanding and personable professional, renewed confidence in the financial figures which began to flow from her office.[91] Nevertheless, the figures were not pretty and they became uglier with each month.

As of 31 March 1991, Cooper reported an accumulated deficit of $2,663,541. This included previously non-budgeted items, such as the faculty lounge, which alone had added close to $200,000 to the debt.[92] A stringent watch was inaugurated over all expenditures. Those responsible for budgets met monthly with Cooper, and the computer system was reprogrammed so that managers could finally receive on-time monthly statements indicating all expenditures both paid and unpaid.[93]

Still figures worsened. Cooper added more unbudgeted items to the deficit, which by June, stood at between $3,000,000 and $3,200,000. By then it was estimated that football had cost $300,000. Cash flow problems were beginning to mount and words like "bankruptcy" and "the end" of UCCB, were heard at general University sessions.[94] Matters could hardly get worse. But they did. It was learned, in early June, that the operating budget from the provincial government for 1991-92 would increase by only one-half of one percent. Since the University College had counted on a 3.5 percent increase, it meant income would be $375,000 less than expected.[95]

Terry and Shannon left for Halifax to plead a case for assistance. They found a government which, though committed to the uniqueness of the institution, would help only if a multi-year financial plan for eliminating the deficit was presented. They were even considering a complete management audit of the University College.[96] This did not solve the immediate financial challenge, so Terry met with bankers while in Halifax—only to discover that their confidence in the institution had been badly shaken: they too wanted a multi-year financial plan.[97]

Within three weeks, Cooper came up with a plan to alleviate the debt within five years, and a copy was immediately sent to the Bank of Nova Scotia. However, the bank not only found the plan unacceptable, but were so concerned with cash-flow problems that they indicated they might not be able to continue banking with the University College. Cooper began working on another plan to please both the board and the bank.[98]

Toward the end of July, Cooper presented her second five-year financial plan to the executive of the board. Its proposals for layoffs, a ten percent tuition increase in its first two years and seven percent afterwards, and a mandatory-retirement program were rejected by union representatives, who went so far as to pass a vote of non-confidence in administration. The Board however, with the bankers at their backs, had no alternative but to accept the plan.[99] Indeed, matters were so bad that there were fears the August payroll could not be met; the province had to move ahead the August grant to the University College so this could happen. Even so, staff were asked to wait two weeks before cashing their August pay cheques. Shannon commented that the institution was performing "a high wire act."[100]

Shannon, meanwhile, had become frustrated with the University College's relationship with the Bank of Nova Scotia and its threat not to renew existing credit. The Board asked six banks, including the Bank of Nova Scotia, to submit financing proposals. Eventually, the Bank of Montreal's proposal was accepted.[101] By the end of August the cash flow was once again solid, the "crunch" was over and monthly budgetary reviews were succeeding in cutting costs.[102]

The problems were far from over, however. The football saga had finally played itself out simultaneously with the financial crisis. After the Board announced the elimination of football in March, J.I. Albrecht's position became redundant and he was dropped from the staff. He announced his intention of taking his case to the courts, but eventually settled for a six-month severance fee.[103] Meanwhile an Athletic Council was planned, with the interim appointment of a new coach, Tim MacGarrigle, and a committee of advisers made up of Jack Porter and Carl "Bucky" Buchanan, of the Athletics Department, and John Terry.[104] At the end of August,

Buchanan returned as head of an Athletics Department with a much restricted varsity program: basketball and hockey.[105]

The final chapter came when the Canadian Inter-University Athletic Union (CIAU) investigated both hockey and football, and in June UCCB had been found guilty of paying tuition, room and board, as well as return airfare for football players. To end the embarrassment, the University College agreed pay a fine of $1,000. In addition, the Athletic Council answered the CIAU's recommendation that unless a proper system to monitor the eligibility of student athletes were implemented, further reviews would take place.[106]

While Albrecht was on his way out, Hill was on his way back. The hearing on Hill's case for wrongful dismissal came before the courts March 19. He alleged that proper process had not been followed: there had not been appropriate notice given for the board meeting at which his dismissal had been discussed; he had not been allowed to address the Board; and the Board had contravened articles of his contract.[107] Despite objections that they did not give the whole picture of the firing, the University College was ordered to hand over to the court the minutes of the meeting that had moved for dismissal.[108]

Though the case was scheduled to be heard May 8-9, the Search Committee continued to seek Hill's replacement, examining the applications of 45 candidates, with finalists to appear before College Council the day before the Hill hearing. That process stalled on two accounts: the Supreme Court found in favour of Hill and, by that date, the Search Committee had failed to recommend a replacement.[109]

The question now became whether or not to appeal the court's decision. All through May and early June the institution's lawyers gave conflicting advice to the Board which debated accepting Hill's return while appealing the court's decision, and perhaps hoping Hill would accept a financial settlement in the meantime. Hill, however, was ready to return, even though John Terry did not seem ready to welcome him, claiming he was still acting president.[110] Indeed, the chairman of the Search Committee,

Irving Schwartz, presented the College Council with three possible presidential candidates for appraisal just as Hill's return seemed certain.[111] Fortunately or unfortunately, they were all rejected.[112]

The community was appalled by the situation. The Alumni and Friends group urged the Board to obey the Supreme Court's decision and called for the resignation of all those who had participated in the decision to fire Hill in the first place.[113] T-shirts popped up with the slogan "GIVE 'EM HELL HILL," in preparation for his return.[114] Some of the faculty of Arts and Science passed yet another resolution, this time calling for Shannon's resignation. The Student Union followed suit a few days later. Shannon shrugged it all off, saying, "There is no chance anyone will resign."[115] This included Hill, who was reinstated in time for the Executive meeting of the Board on June 17, 1991, after being welcomed back by 40 friends and a piper who led him, like a returning Celtic warrior, to his office.[116]

Hill's return did little to quell the air of crisis that hung over the institution during the remainder of 1991. Though a month later the Board decided not to appeal the court's verdict, Hill was far from safe harbour. University college lawyers had openly mused that the technicalities that had saved Hill's job could be corrected and that the board could once again move to fire him if it so desired. There was also the matter of the libellous remarks about Schwartz and Shannon that Hill supposedly made after his firing, specifically concerning Shannon's conflict of interest over University College building contracts, which Shannon had contested and which was still before the courts.[117]

Meanwhile, financial problems continued under threat of bankruptcy and an impending auditor's report. There was also the rankling matter of the "27th pay," which extended back to December 1988. In most years, employees received 26 pay cheques per year, one every two weeks. However, every 10 to 12 years there was an extra or 27th pay, which should have happened in 1988. Despite questions from people like William Gallivan and astute Board members like Greg O'Keefe, administration had refused to pay the amount because Tom MacNeil had not seen this as a potential problem. He had argued that the staff would be over-compensated by two weeks. Besides, the payment would have removed another $300,000 from that year's already-tight budget.[118]

The Nova Scotia Government Employees Union (NSGEU), which represented the technology faculty of the University College, had demanded the pay, taken the matter to arbitration and won their case in September 1990.[119] The University College's lawyer recommended that appeal was futile, so discussions began with NSGEU representatives for reimbursement.[120] By this time, the financial situation of the institution had become perilous, so the Board Committee asked that the Union forgo payment of interest on the amount. This was refused, and payment at 13 percent compound interest demanded, which was unacceptable to the Board who then planned to go back to arbitration in February. Despite a compromise, with payment to be made to NSGEU member employees in March, the University College refused to pay other employees, though they did agree to talks with faculty.[121]

The university faculty, represented by the Canadian Association of University Teachers (CAUT), took legal action to recover the pay. Senior administration met with the University College lawyer and the Negotiating Committee of the Board, with the result that an offer was made to CAUT employees.[122] An offer also made to the administration. This infuriated Shannon, who noted that the Negotiating Committee had no authority to deal with the administration, and he saw this as another case of Hill, now back in office, acting without consulting the Board. Hill cited the morale problems the case was causing, and though it was eventually resolved, the former contention between Hill and Shannon continued.[123]

The annual auditor's report on the University College's finances exposed its problems more forcefully. The accountants, Doane Raymond, revealed the extent to which football had hurt the University College financially, including the writing off of $134,000 in tuition for players, far in excess of the $1,500 allowed by the CIAU. In addition, $37,000 in cash had been paid to hockey and basketball players without tax forms or work to warrant the pay. The authority for this spending was "unclear," but it was bound to reflect on the office of the Vice-President Finance, to which these activities reported. Other matters, such as poor purchasing policies, unregulated travel expenditures, overpayments to the pension plan, expenses far in excess of budget, and gross overestimates of revenues were just as serious, if less sensational. The unforeseen expenses, as in the termination of Hill, or changes in the management of accounting for items, such as the student/faculty lounge or part-time teaching contracts, simply added fuel to the seemingly uncontrolled fire of expenses.[124]

The report was also critical of the way the endowment fund was being handled. This lay squarely with the board's investment committee which agreed that the fund was in "terrible shape," and appeared to be shrinking. The return rate on investments was only 5.3 percent at a time when term deposits were earning eleven percent.[125] A fund manager was quickly hired, the funds were divided between capital and the endowment funds and reinvested, so that between January and June of 1992, the fund was realizing a 13 percent return.[126] As the local president of the University Teachers Faculty Association, Donald MacGillivray noted, "incompetency or very curious accounting practices" seemed to be the rule at all levels of management.[127] A much deeper financial analysis was needed so the board finally decided to ask the Minister of Education for a thorough management audit of all aspects of the operations of the institution, consulting all constituencies of the University College.[128] The process began in December 1991, and ended the following March. During that time more than 100 individuals and groups, from both the University College and the larger community, were interviewed by a team from the Halifax management consultant firm of Peat, Marwick, Stevenson and Kellogg.

As the audit proceeded, even more problems accumulated. Just after the beginning of classes in September, an 18-year-old woman alleged that she had been sexually assaulted in residence by three male students. With no sexual harassment policy or code of residence behaviour in place to deal with such cases, little was immediately done. The president made press statements that the girl and three males had engaged in sex in a residence room. Female faculty and staff representatives then claimed

Hill had sensationalized the incident. The RCMP, which investigated the incident, also raised the ire of many when it was alleged they pressured the girl to change her story, going so far as to charge the girl, who had returned home, with mischief—a charge they soon dropped. A month after the incident, only one male student had been expelled from his position of residence official. Hill could do nothing until the RCMP completed an investigation into its own role in the incident.[129]

In the midst of this controversy, the popular and respected *Maclean's* magazine, in its first ranking of Canadian institutions of higher learning, placed UCCB at the bottom of 46 institutions it surveyed in matters based on the number of top students attracted from outside the region, number of scholarships obtained, endowments, class-size ratios, research, faculty qualifications and facilities. Hill was quick to point out that the University College was new, with thus only a small accumulated endowment, had a policy of accepting lower-ranking students with the aim of improving them, had a large native component, had mainly an island-directed mandate and emphasized "life-long learning."[130] While most fair-minded people agreed with Hill's response, the fact remained that yet another undeserved blow had been struck at morale.

Attempts at belt-tightening continued into the fall, but the anticipation of the management audit overshadowed daily events. In December, the audit group began its work, meeting with the University College community. Members included Richard Criddle, former Vice-President Administration at University of Toronto; Dr. James Downey, past president of the University of New Brunswick; Ken Hubbard, a partner with Peat Marwick and expert in Human Resource Management; and Robbie Shaw, project leader and former Vice-President Finance and Administration at Dalhousie University. As far as anyone knew, this was the first such in-depth study of any Canadian university.[131] Such a study, later to be known as the Shaw-Downey report, would be extensive in any institution, but because the University College's financial crisis, rapid growth, unusual composition, and mandate demanded even greater analysis and reform.

The committee soon realized that the University College organization had not kept up with either its growth or its mandate. Its growth had outpaced most post-secondary institutions in the previous ten years; but it still operated like its predecessor, the liberal arts Junior College, with few written policies, governed by a few members of senior management who controlled the budget and dominated the Board with little direct accountability, and who held "appointments for life." It had never even formulated a mission statement or a comprehensive set of goals and objectives.[132] The result was that people did not feel part of the governance process and morale was low, or as the report stated, a "general malaise" had settled over the University College.[133]

The report recommended that to boost the sense of ownership of the institution, a general openness was needed; the Board and Academic Council (formerly College Council) meetings should be open to the public except on very confidential matters.[134] To increase the participation of the total Board in the operation of the institution, orientation sessions explaining their various roles should be held with faculty and administrators. The downsized Board should meet more regularly, with more student representatives, but fewer political appointees and only one representative of senior administration, namely the president. This would eliminate management's domination of the board, whose members should in turn realize that they should not interfere in the day-to-day operation of the University College. In other words, the Board should set major policies, approve budgets and investments, direct legal affairs, for which the institution should retain a solicitor, and act as a buffer between the university and the community.[135]

During meetings of the Board in January and February of 1992, both the Academic Vice-President, William Gallivan, and Tom MacNeil announced they would step down from their positions that year, the latter going into retirement. The investigators felt this was an opportunity to eliminate the position of Academic Vice-President, ensuring that the president would be the Chief Academic Officer, with the deans reporting directly to that office. In turn, the deans should take responsibility for academic planning, including the faculty budget. This would ensure accountability, as department heads would have to articulate their budget requirements to the deans and coordinate the participation of faculty in the student advisory process. They also suggested that consideration be given to replacing the position of Vice-President Finance and administration with a Director Of Finance and Administration.[136]

The final aspect of governance dealt with Academic Council, which, along with the Board, governed the University College in a bi-cameral fashion. The investigating team discovered that the council's role had diminished over the years. In fact, it was not even mentioned in the Act of Incorporation of 1974. It was seen as irrelevant, with most active and powerful committees, such as planning and priorities, reporting to the board. To strengthen it, the president should serve as its chair, other administrators should be called to meetings only when needed as advisors, and at times it should meet jointly with the board of governors.[137]

Finances were obviously a main focus of concern. The team felt that the power of the administration to spend money without having it, reflected a weak, fractioned financial administration acting without controls or policies. It found that in the years 1986-91, teaching and academic non-teaching costs had risen by 34 percent, physical plant costs by 9.5 percent, but administrative and general expenses by 150 percent.[138] It concluded that operating costs should be tied to the ability to pay and the institutes, research, and ancillary services should pay their own way or at least recover expenses. As well, the institution should charge for parking, admission to the Playhouse and the Art Gallery.[139]

Guidelines, as well as written job descriptions and policies for all departments and sectors were needed, including research and fund raising. Added to this, the envelope concept of financial management was to be inaugurated, whereby each budget manager would have financial responsibility along with spending authority. If to this were added a Finance Committee of the Board of Governors to oversee all financial aspects of the institution, supported by upgraded computer software services, the budget would be made "real" for the first time.[140]

During its encounters with members of the University College community, the team was struck by the low morale caused by the feeling that money was being wasted, and the lack of understanding between its two teaching arms, represented by two distinct unions. It was first of all obvious a human resources management department was needed to clarify the collective bargaining process, and supply policy guidelines so that people were certain of the rights of management and employees.[141]

But this was not enough. The institution was like a "duplex partitioned by misperceptions and mistrust." Little or no progress had been made in the difficult job of integrating the academic and technology cultures, and

> if UCCB continues on its present course, it seems likely that its degree programs will continue to resemble other liberal arts universities and its diploma programs will continue to resemble other community colleges. The appropriateness of this strategy in a province containing 13 universities and 18 community colleges is questionable.[142]

The very layout of the institution militated against interaction of the technology and academic sectors. The former "C" wing of the campus became the "territory" of the Trades and Technology faculty with separate classes and laboratories, though often the same faculty taught both. The Trades sector was even more isolated, since it fell under the jurisdiction of the Department of Labour rather than Education. Trades students learned nothing about such subjects as the history of trade unions or how to operate a trades-based business even though the history and business departments boasted experts in those fields. An opportunity to create a new integrated way of learning had been neglected.[143] A change in direction was obviously needed to integrate the two cultures in a single faculty with the four schools headed by deans and department heads with real power and leadership. The department heads, as presently constituted, were seen by the team as "glorified secretaries."[144]

The team also felt that as long as there were two separate unions for the teaching staff, a sufficient spirit of collegiality and single purpose would not likely be achieved. A single faculty union could be backed by a comprehensive agreement, which the university did not yet have. Rank and tenure, as well, should reflect the founding value of the institution and trends in thinking in post-secondary education, with more weight given to teaching excellence and community contribution, and less to research. Awards should be given to recognize a job well done in those areas, along with performance goals and teaching feedback.[145]

As far as students were concerned, the team recommended that:

> A customer service mind set should be instituted in all university staff so that it is clearly understood that students are the basic reason for the existence of the institution rather than being treated as a commodity. [146]

This was a stinging indictment of past attitudes, which could only be rectified by increasing student independence, hiring a Dean of Student Services separate from the Human Resources director, as well as grievance officers for student complaints. Students should sit on governing committees, receive better orientation, be subject to a Student Union judicial system, and participate in course evaluations in order to better choose courses. Student horizons should be broadened and contacts made off-island by affiliating the Student Union with the Student Union of Nova Scotia and the Canadian Federation of Students.[147] While varsity sports were good for school spirit, intramural sports were probably a "more valuable contribution to the regular day-to-day student life," and a recommendation was made for a Student Services Committee to "have a look" at the possibility of broadening intramural sports programs.[148]

Though the physical plant was the target of constant complaints, the team surprisingly found its operation satisfactory and cost-effective, and questioned the need for more space if facilities could be more efficiently used. Nonetheless, it suggested a specialized in-depth space analysis.[149]

Beyond the institution, the University College was found to be a leader in providing community direction, but the study felt this role had been allowed to diminish during the 80s, reflecting the fact that it was losing site of its original mandate. The irony was that other universities not only envied UCCB's community role, but were moving to emulate it. The team agreed that the location of the campus was a "serious error," but closer ties with municipal authorities, a strengthened alumni board, improved relations with areas outside industrial Cape Breton, and better communications with the AVTC could go a long way to put the institution back on track. It was recommended that the Director of Public Relations prepare a strategic communications plan.[150]

The consultants acknowledged that such a massive overhaul not only of personnel, but of attitudes and practices, seemed a daunting task, but it could be accomplished by a strategic planning policy which in the past had been haphazard to say the least, given the fact that the University College had had three very different presidents in the tumultuous past three and one-half years. The process should start within a year, however, and be undertaken by a "bottom-up" standing committee of the Academic Council, chosen by the president and reporting to the Board.[151]

Until this was undertaken, as one student put it, "Walking about this place [would do] nothing to counter the tendency of Cape Bretoners to think poorly of themselves."[152] The changes to counter this attitude were possible, the team felt, but "the greater danger for UCCB is that it may continue to expect too little of itself, that its grasp may fall short of its reach."[153]

The Shaw-Downey Report was released March 19, 1992. President Hill returned from a visit with his family in the little town of Canning, Nova Scotia and, having previously read parts of the report, quickly resigned. "I think it's the right decision for the institution ... I realized the university has had enough controversy and maybe I should resign, I did not want to be seen as a roadblock."[154] Though the report did not lay major blame for the problems at UCCB on him, looking back, he admitted: "Hindsight is a good thing and mistakes were made along the way but I've been a risk taker and sometimes those risks don't all turn out."[155]

Shannon blamed no-one in particular for the university college's problems, placing it at the foot of everyone, from the Board to administration and faculty, for years of not "paying attention. We should have done some navel gazing sooner."[156]

Top management was practically stripped away, from Hill and MacNeil to Gallivan and, finally, John Terry, who decided to give up the job of Acting President. The Executive of the Board, depending on his experience and breadth of vision, asked Gallivan to accept the position as interim president until a new president could be found. Gallivan felt that he had no choice in the matter and that his decision would not be popular because, to many, he represented "the old boys' network."[157] He was right. The unionized faculty and staff, after a vituperative ninety-minute session condemned the way he was selected and called the appointment unacceptable.[158] Gallivan, never known for his faint-heartedness, bluntly retorted, "I've never lost sight of my responsibility that in the absence of the president, I act in his place." He did not see the selection of an interim president as a popularity contest: "that has never been a driving force in my life and I've made tough decisions in the past and I say that with pride." [159] Gallivan also had to contend with Shannon for whom he had little regard. The feeling seemed mutual and Gallivan indicates that Shannon unsuccessfully sought an outside candidate to fill the position.[160] Once he was appointed, however, the majority of the Board stood by Gallivan. On the advice of James Foulds of the Biology Department, Gallivan met with a group of faculty to get their advice and support. This collegial move helped temper the discord between faculty and administration and probably accounts for some of the relative peace during the ensuing six months.[161]

Despite Board support, the pressure on Gallivan was gruelling; all the more reason to speed up the presidential search. While a committee of the Academic Council and another made up of the Board, students, faculty and community representatives studied the Shaw-Downey Report, agreeing and disagreeing with parts of it, it was obvious that full implementation would have to wait until a new president was appointed.[162] Accordingly, a presidential committee was struck in May, headed by local popular community-involved business person, Selma Rudderham, with student, faculty, and Board representation.[163]

Although the period of Gallivan's tenure and the presidential search could have been one of almost suspended animation, closer examination reveals that this was far from the case, and that a surprising agility was shown by the University College to move on and accept change despite adversity. In June, a student judicial system was adopted based on the recommendations of the Shaw-Downey Report.[164] In August, four new deans were appointed, indicating final acceptance of Hill's four-school structure. Appointees were popular members of faculty: Bill Clemens, as Dean of Arts and Social Sciences; David White, as Dean of Applied Arts and Development Studies; John Coleman of the faculty of Trades and Technology as Dean of Business; and Lino Polegato, former Director of Engineering, as Dean of Science and Technology.[165]

As well, the budget estimates reflected a serious belt-tightening resulting in a predicted surplus in August of $600,000 for the coming year. Indeed, the institution had already reached its first five-year goal of reducing the budget by $300,000 in 1991-92. "We've clearly turned the corner," Gallivan exulted.[166] Even Shannon cautiously commented, "we are doing much better than last year," to the tune of $800,000 in savings by October.[167] It is significant that Shannon made this statement at the Board's first public meeting, implementing yet another of the Audit Committee's recommendations.

Other events were also developing, quite unrelated to the Shaw-Downey Report, that boded well. In June 1990, a letter of understanding had been obtained from the University of Waterloo, agreeing to have some of its doctoral students perform their research in conjunction with UCCB.[168] This resulted in a close relationship between the two institutions, which saw George Soulis from Waterloo helping to develop a Memorandum of Understanding (MOU) between the University College and Enterprise Cape Breton (ECB), the federal government's regional economic authority, to act as a "support network to entrepreneurship."[169] Soulis formed strong links with the Research and Development department and, together with ECB, a plan evolved to help UCCB in its efforts to deal with technological development in Cape Breton.[170] This was accompanied by the announcement in April 1991 that the University College had won a prestigious and valuable combined Natural Sciences and Engineering Research and Social Sciences Research Council (NSERC/SSHRC) grant for the establishment of a Chair in the Management of Technological Change, thanks to the efforts of Gregory MacLeod of the Tompkins Institute. The Chair included funding for graduate student research as well as a director and represented the first major NSERC/SSHRC grant to the University College, one that was unusual for so small an institution.[171] Its effects, together with the MOU, would have a profound effect on the institution and Cape Breton.

By May of 1992, the MOU had generated twenty research projects, and the NSERC/SSHRC grants were over $180,000 excluding the $500,000 that had been made as the first installment towards the establishment of the Chair. Research was now focused on technology; to this was added the environment, with a faculty committee on Applied Research on the Environment. Even the Environmental Services Laboratory, which Hill had inaugurated in 1990 to analyze chemicals found in the environment, including Sydney's Tar Ponds, for which he had been criticized, and which had been losing money, was stabilized with help from the MOU and the work of its director, Jim Wilson, was beginning to see its revenue grow, thus saving it from threatened closure.[172]

Coincidental with these events, the new residence was opened by Premier Cameron. Sod was also turned for a new building for expanded classrooms, offices, a bookstore and a sports heritage centre. Despite these signs of renewal, a feeling of discontent still pervaded the University College during the fall term of 1992. William Gallivan brought some reassurance when he told the press that the powerful Nova Scotia Council for Higher Education saw UCCB as "an extremely important factor in the future cultural and economic development of this island and have a strong commitment to our university."[173] The University College and the community could be forgiven for thinking they had heard this many times before and with no financial follow-through. In reality, the future of the institution would depend on how well it carried out the recommendations of the Shaw-Downey Report which awaited the appointment of a new president.

VII

Renewed Vision, 1993-2002

The fifth decade of the development of UCCB occurred in much the same context as earlier ones: the local economy, population, and government share of funding continued to decline, while enrolment, programs and the size of the physical plant continued to expand. During the presidency of Jacquelyn Thayer Scott, creative methods were developed to meet the resulting threats to the institution's survival, but a pattern developed under the preceding presidents persisted: a period of optimism, followed by internal conflict, disillusion and resignations.

Institutional changes recommended in the Shaw-Downey Report awaited the appointment of a new president. A Search Committee made up of nine local Board members, which included faculty and students, began the process in May 1992. The 34 applicants were narrowed to four and then to two after meeting with the College Council, newly-

Fig. 9. Photo by Paul Prendergast. Stone fence, the "Dingwall," @ 1995. Beaton Institute of Cape Breton Studies, University College of Cape Breton. 95-497-26588.

renamed Academic Council. The search committee's recommendation of Jacquelyn Thayer Scott was accepted by the Board October 30.[1] She took up her duties January 1, and was formally installed April 29, 1993.[2] Scott's six-year contract included, unlike Hill's, academic tenure.[3]

Scott was certainly aware of the problems of the university, but she was attracted to Cape Breton. Its distinctiveness, and the concept of a new kind of institution of higher learning in the midst of an industrial economy appealed to her. Besides, crisis management was one of her areas of research.[4] While the board expected her to "heal the wounds and open the president's office," she was soon made aware that the province was planning to rationalize higher education and that "UCCB might cease to exist and become a satellite campus for one of the other universities up the line."[5] There had been rumours, a few years old, that "some in the province have suggested that ... UCCB should be stripped of its university status and revert to some less ambitious role in the island community."[6] To prevent this, Scott had to "get the community back on side and get ourselves out of the deficit," and "develop what made the institution unique: the notion of the university college," which some faculty had never accepted. Yet, only by faculty co-operation and fiscal responsibility could the University College "buy its freedom."[7]

She had no illusions as to expect help from Halifax: "When you're in our position, you weren't going to get more money anyway so you better manage what you have well and succeed in spite of them."[8] Failing further financial aid from the provincial government, Scott soon concluded that federal funding agencies provided an option. The problem was that the University College was unknown to them. She therefore decided to undertake a long-term strategy of enlightening Ottawa as to the existence and uniqueness of the institution. She obtained appointments to various influential boards involving science and research funding. This, she hoped, would raise the University College's profile and in turn lead to the province's providing fairer funding.[9]

Part of any success in these areas rested on putting into effect the reforms suggested by the Shaw-Downey report, including a five-year strategic plan which Scott inaugurated in the first month of her presidency as a joint Academic Council and Board committee, to report in November.[10] Other Shaw-Downey proposals were put into practice even before the plan's adoption. The first public meeting of the Board had taken place in October 1992 with an information session on the institutes and their role in the community, heralding a greater public openness on the part of the institution. In addition, student influence was soon increased with representation on the executive of the Board.[11]

The impending changes at UCCB also had to be placed in the context of provincial demands. Premier Donald Cameron, in an effort to rationalize efforts and save money, had ordered universities to end program duplication and develop a plan designating specialties among them. He warned if they could not do so, he would do it for them.[12] This stand was underlined by Janet Halliwell, Chair of the Nova Scotia Council for Higher Education, who was commissioned to plan the restructuring of Nova Scotia's universities. In line with Cameron's orders, each institution had to update its Role and Planned Capacity Statement by March. Since this coincided with UCCB's ongoing strategic planning process, the Council agreed to extend UCCB's deadline to October, so that its own role and planned capacity statement could be interpreted in the light of its strategic plan.[13]

The University College Strategic Planning Committee planned to make public its report in November. The group's steering committee, chaired by the president, included members of Academic Council, the Board, Student Union, and staff associations. It created six sub-committees: Academic Programs and Research, Community Life, Outreach, Human Resources, Buildings and Grounds and Enrolment/Recruitment. Internal dialogues were held with every department as well as with 36 external constituencies all over Cape Breton Island, more than 550 questionnaires were received from students, more than 130 comments from alumni, and a further 121 comments by mail, phone and fax from the general public. The thoroughness of the process was likely without precedent in the Canadian post-secondary system.[14]

In March, the Steering Committee met in Baddeck to discuss the general course of the University College in the ensuing years. The resulting plan played an important role in shaping the eventual mission statement which would allow the institution "to actively shape its future rather than watching it be shaped by others."[15]

The mission statement of the final report boldly stated the centrality of the university college concept, "which reflects, integrates and develops the liberal arts, sciences, technologies, and trades traditions." Following the Shaw-Downey Report's recommendations, it emphasized the "diversity and centrality of students," as well as the "special partnership with the peoples, cultures and communities of Cape Breton...." These elements were the essence of the mission statement, rooted in the earliest traditions of the institution and now formally adopted by the Board of Governors.[16]

The seven goals and objectives which followed from this mission, dealt with quality and excellence in teaching, research, accessibility, the learning environment as well as the actions which the University College must take to meet the rapid changes taking place in the educational environment. But the first goal was "to recognize and express our unique structure and mandate through a fully comprehensive range of excellent academic programs."[17]

UCCB's role and planned capacity statement followed directly from the Strategic Plan and was presented to the Nova Scotia Council of Higher Education (NSCHE) in December 1993. Following this, representatives of NSCHE visited the University College to begin the program assessment with the view of eliminating program duplication. The overall impression was positive. Indeed, Scott reported that after a thorough study, the institution had "emerged almost unscathed" from the review of the province's thirteen degree-granting institutions. UCCB had indeed carved out its own niche in the university system.[18]

While NSCHE evaluated and approved courses, structural changes took place in 1993-94, also in line with recommendations of the Shaw-Downey Report. The joint academic council/board committee, organized to discuss and recommend changes to the university college's organization, suggested reforms that aroused a great deal of emotion. The powers of the president however, remained essentially unchanged as well as those of the academic schools of Arts and Letters, Community Studies, Science and Technology and Business, with their various departments. The placement of some departments such as Politics, Government and Public Administration in the School of Community Studies, and Behavioural and Life Sciences, which included psychology, in the School of Science and Technology, caused some controversy but, on the whole, Peter Hill's earlier vision of the schools system was being adopted. Its blending of science and technology in one school, underlined the board's hope the "Institutions' real strength would be developed out of both traditions, leading to important teaching and research activity."[19]

Along with the formal acceptance of the schools system, a peer review committee for academic advancement, a Professional Development Committee for the management of research and sabbaticals awards, and an Appeals Committee were eventually established.[20]

Perhaps the most controversial area was the role of Academic Council. Originally known as College Council, its role had been advisory to the president in academic areas including financial resources, relating to course development, though this role had declined in the 80s, leaving it to deal with purely academic matters, such as course and program changes. At the time of the financial crisis, the Board was curtly reminded by earlier members, including former president, D.F. Campbell and past Chair of the Board of Governors, Denne Burchell, that Council was meant to be made aware of financial matters, so that they could have an input into the affairs of the institution. The former members added that since Council had lost that ability, faculty and community perceived it as powerless, which in turn led to faculty and community protests witnessed in such groups as the "Friends of UCCB." They asked that some responsibilities be restored so that Council could perform its original purpose.[21]

It was hoped that this strengthening of Academic Council would rejuvenate the bi-cameral nature of the University College's governance. Reforms that followed gave a larger role to members in the budgetary process, but, contrary to the recommendations of the Shaw-Downey report, the president was not made chairperson; instead, senior faculty members were to be chosen and the number of faculty representatives was increased to outnumber those from administration. As well, senior administrators sat *ex-officio,* in contradistinction to the recommendations of the report.[22]

As well, the Report's recommendation of a single faculty association combining all teaching staff, academic and technological, in order to break down the disciplinary barriers was rejected. Faculty were firm in their wish to retain separate unions, one for the liberal arts academics (the Faculty Association of University Teachers or FAUT) and one for trades and technology faculty (Nova Scotia Government Employees Union or NSGEU).[23]

The latter, however, supported the new structure but the academic staff had more problems, especially with the repeal of the bylaws governing the faculties.[24] The bylaws had to be replaced, since legal council had warned that the former faculty of Arts and Science bylaws were not really a formal agreement in writing between the University College and FAUT, and were therefore not a collective agreement according to the Trade Union Act.[25] The student representatives on the Board meanwhile, joined in supporting the new structure and bylaws.[26]

Finally, in formal recognition of the new structure and the growing maturity of the institution, John T. McLennan, president of Bell Canada, and a Cape Bretoner, was appointed chancellor.[27] A Port Hood jeweller, Daryl MacLeod, designed a mace and a chain of office for the chancellor; Leo MacNeil, a Sydney area furniture designer fashioned two oak chairs for the chancellor and vice-chancellor, who was also the president.[28]

New deans were appointed to lead the schools: Thomas Rendell as Dean of Arts and Letters; Steve Manley returning as Dean of Science and Technology; Steve Kavanagh, Dean of School of Business; and Silver Donald Cameron, as Dean of Community Studies.[29] As well, and in recognition of the growing focus on students, David White was appointed head of the newly organized Department of Student Services.[30]

The new "flattened" structure, without vice-presidents between the senior administrators and the president, followed the recommendations of the Shaw-Downey Report. However, with so many deans, directors and the chief librarian all reporting to the president, there was the danger that communications would become unwieldy, to say the least. Scott wanted to set up a management team that could not only draw all these threads together, but also produce much-needed policies on everything from research ethics to residence management, sexual harassment, and budgetary procedures. She therefore decided to have the deans meet on a regular basis in what was first called a Dean's Advisory Council (DAC), to discuss common concerns and to advise the president. To give cohesion to the group, the former Dean of Extension and Community Affairs, Raymond Ivany, was appointed Dean of Institutional Affairs and assistant to the president.[31] He chaired DAC meetings, sat as secretary to the Board, smoothed interschool relations, interrelated closely with the president and, in many cases, became the voice of the president in the day-to-day operations of the University College. This also gave Scott time to pursue connections outside the institution. Much of the success of the internal operations of the institution in the next six years was attributable to the hard work and political acumen of this earnest administrator.[32] Eventually other senior administrators entered the group which became known as the President's Advisory Council (PAC).[33] The group's restricted nature raised suspicions in some quarters as to its being a "rat PAC," serving as a threatening parallel structure to Academic Council or the Board. Though it had no formally delegated powers or existence, under Ivany's tutelage it played an important role in administrative efficiency. In effect, PAC reflected Scott's innovative attitude toward university administration. As she noted:

> At other institutions there is a split between academic and administrative managers and an inequality between the two. What we did was put all the people responsible for the various functional areas into one group to build a team. The deans are at the same table as the director for buildings and grounds.[34]

PAC certainly did become an interactive body which, for the first time since the formation of the University College, brought administrators together for a common cause in management efficiency. Scott hoped this would move people away from their traditional loyalty primarily to their discipline or profession to that of the University College as a whole.[35] Under Ivany, PAC's activities grew to include budget and policy development. With his direct link to the president and the Board, the latter was kept in contact with administrative concerns and developments. As well, members of PAC regularly addressed the Board on the areas under their direction. This ensured that the Board and senior administration were kept informed of each other's activities, would develop mutual confidence, and avoid previous crises of trust. This probably accounts for the good relations between the Board and the administration. Though both strong-minded people, Shannon and Scott had common goals and worked well together, ending the old problem of jurisdictional wrangling.[36] Yet this solidarity had unfortunate consequences at other levels of the university college; many faculty believed that "good relations" were between administrators at the expense of academic responsibilities, driving a wedge between the executive branch and the front lines of the institution.

As changes in line with the recommendations of the Shaw-Downey report and the strategic plan proceeded, the University College entered a period of remarkable growth. The enthusiasm generated by a new, imaginative president and a new road map, encouraged most members of the University College community to leave behind the crises and confusion of the past and to "rise again." The future held enough challenges without these added burdens. With the 1990s came changing trends in the makeup of the student body. The economic situation in Industrial Cape Breton continued to worsen and, with rising tuitions and a decrease in the number of local high school students, there was a real danger of declining enrolment. Between 1996 and 1998, the Cape Breton-Victoria Regional School board lost 1,600 students, the Strait Regional, at the west end of the island, 400 students.[37] In 1993, 89 percent of the students at UCCB were local; this number had only dropped to 85 percent in 1998, despite the attempt to recruit off-island students. Indeed, the increase in enrolment of international students looks impressive—up 64.7 percent, but the actual numbers were quite small.

Overall enrolment remained relatively stable, however, despite the crises the institution had endured. Numbers had grown from 2,872 full-time to 3,369 between 1989 and 1992.[38] The number thereafter evened off with a two percent increase in 1997, but a decline of 3.4 percent to 3,414 in 1998.[39] While this decline was marginal in comparison to some other universities, there was a realization that the administration, especially the registrar's office, along with faculty and students must increase recruitment efforts.[40] Visits were made to high schools throughout the region as well as to western Newfoundland. Notwithstanding some success, the decline continued: 50 fewer students in 1999, a 9.9 percent drop in 2000, one percent in 2001. By 2002, however, forecasts called for a considerable increase in enrolment.[41]

While regular full-time enrolment fluctuated, the off-campus programs showed rapid expansion. In 1990, the Extension and Community Affairs Department (ECA), began "stand-alone" credit courses throughout the island, which did not necessarily lead to a degree. Within two years courses were being taught by adjunct faculty in business, the humanities, and the social sciences, and enrolment was up by 120 percent. Along with specialized programs for teachers, "non-traditional students" over 25 years of age were also following courses and programs. Interactive video conferencing and satellite teleconferencing were now offered. Not only did these courses make the university a twelve month operation, but they went a long way in bringing UCCB to the community in fulfillment of advice in the Downey report, and indeed harkening back to the early days of the institution. Popular summer courses encouraging science, technology, and entrepreneurship for students in grades eight and nine, heralded a new approach to education and community development.[42] In 1995, ECA launched a unique national education program designed solely for steelworkers.[43]

More dramatically, ECA linked with the Nunavut Arctic College allowing their students to complete science and technology studies at UCCB. The fact that the university and college were under one roof appealed to students seeking a seamless education. Simultaneously, the Centre for International Studies entered a similar agreement with Malaysian business students.[44]

The University College, evolving new approaches, was changing its character; student numbers could no longer be gauged by on-campus registration alone. However, with the increase in off-island students, a second residence (later known as Cabot Residence) was opened in the fall of 2000; a $4,500,000, four-storey building next to the MacDonald Residence which doubled student accommodation with 124 more bedrooms.[45]

It was Scott's conviction that part of the institution's hope for survival and growth lay in new programs and greater breadth of offerings, which was borne out by the attraction of students to the numerous innovative programs added to the curriculum.[46] Many of these programs rested on the strengths of the University College structure and its role in the community. Another development encouraged this tactic. The Maritime Province's Higher Education Commission (MPHEC), which traditionally had to approve regional university programs before they were funded, had not received new money for a number of years. As a result, its role was weakened and universities began offering programs without its approval. This was seen as a green light for the offering of innovative programs. For example, internal approval was given to the offering of the Bachelor of Technology in Environmental Health, Bachelor of Technology in Nautical Sciences and in Chemical Sciences, the Bachelor of Community Studies with a concentration in health and the environment, a diploma in Petroleum Engineering Technology and a Bachelor of Technology in Petroleum Studies.[47]

While traditional academic programs were improved, introducing honours degrees in fields such as Political Science and Communication, non-traditional programs attracted more attention. In 1997, a three-year diploma program in Motive Power Technology was introduced to meet the needs of automobile automation. This program rested upon the University College's unique blend of technology and management skills.[48] The University College also took the lead in the practical development of job readiness skills. A Career Education and Placement Centre was inaugurated to develop placement opportunities for students in Co-op work experience programs. By 1996, the Centre was placing 1,000 students annually.[49]

Community development became the focus of many new programs. In 1998, the degree of Bachelor of Science Community Studies, a combination of liberal arts and sciences and technology, was introduced to focus on community issues with a scientific base, such as the Sydney Tar Ponds. This degree was different from the traditional, more generalized Bachelor of Arts Community Studies and focused on specific areas of research. One area of particular interest to Scott was the University College's specialization in Mi'kmaq Studies. The Mi'kmaq Science Advantage Program, which eventually led to the unique Integrative Science Program, was developed by Professor Cheryl Bartlett in close co-operation with the Mi'kmaq community. As well, a BA/BACS major in

Mi'kmaq Studies was approved in 2001.[50] By 1999, UCCB was educating more aboriginal students annually than any other educational institution in eastern Canada.[51]

In addition, after two years of deliberation, a Master of Business Administration, Community Economic Development, was finally approved in 1998. This program headed by Gertrude MacIntyre, crystallized the role of the University College in the economically hard-pressed community and put UCCB at the forefront of community economic development education in Canada.[52] The institution's Centre for Community Economic Development (CED Institute) was the first community economic development agent in Canada to gain full accreditation to the certified economic development program for the Council for the Advancement of Native Development Officers.

Co-operation with other universities in program development helped break down the isolation of the University College, allowing its expansion into programs which would not otherwise be within reach of local students. One such program was nursing. It had long been hoped to introduce nursing education back to the Island, but St Francis Xavier University taught these courses, and duplication was out of the question. President Scott, with Dr. Ronald Stewart, Minister of Health, developed a collaborative model allowing nursing students to take science programs in both institutions.[53] The program was slated to educate 25 students per year over five years, with the first graduates to enter the workplace in 2003.

Another important example of inter-university cooperation was seen in engineering. UCCB, with the province's largest engineering faculty outside Halifax, allied itself with the Technical University of Nova Scotia (TUNS), allowing engineering students to take their first two years of study locally and complete the last two years at TUNS. Non-engineering students could also take their first two years in Sydney before transferring to TUNS for their final three years.[54]

All this updating of programs at the University College reawakened the old problem of space. Trailers, popularly known as "ATCO Hall," had been installed on campus, at a cost of $70,000, to handle student overflow and office needs.[55] New quality space, however, required new money and the provincial government of Premier Donald Cameron, was in no mood to add to the provincial debt. Instead, just after the accession of Scott to her new position, Cameron decided that he could supply more space to UCCB and save money by amalgamating it with the adjacent Adult Vocational Training Centre (AVTC). The Centre, with a staff of 25 permanent and 15 casual instructors and 750 students, occupied an approximately 200,000 square foot building on an adjoining 3.5 hectare (8.5 acre) campus.[56]

The seemingly large amount of unused space at the AVTC had long held an attraction for the growing University College. The provincial government had toyed with the idea of some sort of integration of the two institutions, and in 1990 the University College had received permission to occupy three to five rooms at the AVTC for three years.[57] President Hill had even proposed to Minister of Education Joel Matheson that UCCB should take charge of the whole college system in Cape Breton, including the AVTC and the Nautical Institute in Port Hawkesbury. This offered the dazzling prospect of saving money, ending course duplications and providing bridging programs between technology, technical trades and university level courses, as well as providing more space for UCCB.[58]

With the spectre of UCCB's three-year tenure of AVTC space coming to an end, in 1993, the provincial government asked the Nova Scotia Council of Higher Education (NSCHE) to investigate the amalgamation of the two institutions. The Council and Cabinet were at once very impressed by the University College's new-found efficiency in financial and academic affairs. At the same time, they recognized the unfairness of formula funding which "at the moment ... is a flat allotment of money which is not based on anything that is terribly rational," according to Janet Halliwell, chair of NSCHE.[59] They also admired the convergence of programs at UCCB, and felt the amalgamation with AVTC would build on the UCCB tradition. Such a funding revision and amalgamation would be the first step in the rationalization of the post-secondary system.[60]

Any unification would quite properly take a period of discussion and debate, but with a provincial election approaching, Cameron wanted to move quickly and demonstrate a commitment to the "marriage." Despite his feeling that "revolution rather than evolution is always unpleasant," he decided to announce the merger.[61]

So, in early April 1993, Cameron came to Sydney to make the announcement and caught everyone off guard. Not only had Scott barely taken office, but the University College's strategic planning process had just begun. Even Joe Shannon, Chairman of the Board, had received only twenty-four hours notice of the announcement, leaving him no time to inform many board members.[62] Cameron indicated that a transition team would be appointed under Halliwell. Direct implementation was to be under the direction of Raymond Ivany for UCCB and Michael MacNeil for AVTC, with Scott given authorization to formulate a merger agreement.[63]

Reaction was alarming. Hundreds of AVTC students "swarmed" Cameron outside the UCCB boardroom, protesting the move and joining others disclaiming the recent announcement of the closure of the nearby Donkin-Morien District High School. The spectre of "people shouting obscenities and brandishing pickets [trying] to shove through the crowd and rush the ... campus police in the doorway leading to the boardroom," had to have startled the premier.[64]

To inflame the situation even more, a UCCB sign was placed over the AVTC entrance a few days later. Students at both institutions protested against the process. Halliwell, however, was firm: "The decision has been made, the amalgamation will proceed ... the real work of the transition will be done over the next year."[65] With a provincial election looming, the whole episode threatened to become a political football. A document from bureaucrats in the Education Department advising against the move was leaked to the press. It predicted that amalgamation would result in no increase in training space for UCCB, increase the tuition for AVTC students and reduce teaching time for most AVTC courses from 215 to 160 days.[66]

It was not long before opposition parties jumped in, condemning the merger as a "corporate takeover," comparing its capriciousness to Cameron's sudden removal of the toll booths at the Canso Causeway the previous year.[67] The premier tried to explain his reasoning to students at a suburban church hall, but was shouted down. The voluble Cameron in turn shouted back, "You are not going to bulldoze me."[68] The day before, Dr. Ron Stewart, Liberal candidate for Cape Breton North, had announced that, if elected, his party would review the merger.[69]

The AVTC students, with the support of the opposition parties, staged a large rally calling for the scrapping of the idea. Douglass Grant, chair of the faculty of Arts and Science at UCCB, condemned the idea, and even suggested, that in light of the fact that the provincial government had withdrawn trades training funding from UCCB, it would be a better idea to merge AVTC with the UCCB trades program, strengthening AVTC and freeing up space at UCCB for classrooms and laboratories.[70]

The provincial election of May 25, 1993, swept the Cameron government from power and shortly after, Premier John Savage announced that the merger was on hold.[71] The new Minister of Education, John MacEachern, set up a ministerial amalgamation review committee to examine the matter.[72] The Committee was composed of MacEachern, the Deputy Minister of Education, Armand Picard, Janet Halliwell, Jacquelyn Scott, and Joe Shannon. They appointed Teresa MacNeil, a troubleshooter from St Francis Xavier University, as a policy advisor. She worked with Vincent Cunningham of the Department of Trades and Technology at UCCB and Charles Muggah of AVTC to examine the feasibility of an alignment of their programs which might eliminate duplication.[73]

Within two weeks MacNeil had reported to the ministerial committee.[74] The committee seemed to favour a federation that would allow both institutions to retain their distinctive features while operating under a single governing body. Most administrative functions could be centralized and the physical plants shared.[75]

The AVTC students would have none of it and were determined to make their voices heard. Noisy rallies were held, attacking UCCB for trying to make up for its poor management by trying to "steal" their institution to pay off its debt.[76] The amalgamation was quietly shelved, having upset the University College community just as it was recovering from earlier crises and grappling with the development of its strategic plan. The strategic plan was, however, accepted and the institution soon began the implementation of its mission.

At the same time, the provincial government continued its examination of the community colleges which resulted in widespread course revisions.[77] The process led to the elimination of outdated courses and the addition or upgrading of many others. In 1996, UCCB and the Nova Scotia Community Colleges signed an unprecedented agreement allowing the full transfer of credits between the two institutions. By that time, the University College had already signed similar agreements with schools in New Brunswick, Newfoundland & Labrador, and Ontario.[78] Such co-operation did a good deal to erase the anger of the past, while revealing UCCB as a national leader in innovative educational cooperation.

But to Scott and many others, this still left the University College overcrowded, with a high-school-like appearance—and a dirty one at that. Discussions on the expansion of the Campus Centre had begun shortly after the occupation of the new campus in 1989 when Peter Hill, following the promises of the provincial government, optimistically hoped a $5,000,000 expansion could begin in 1991, but provincial funding was not forthcoming and the institution's debt was too high to manage on its own.[79]

Instead, a space study was undertaken to determine if available space was being used properly. The Toronto firm hired found that classroom utilization at any one time amounted to only 60 percent of available space and that 75 percent utilization could be achieved, greatly diminishing the need for expansion.[80] Those figures convinced the Board executive to postpone plans for new construction, and immediate attempts were made to change class schedules and free up labs which would otherwise have remained unused.[81] The staff, however, disagreed with the report which they felt had failed to anticipate the growth needs of the campus. While some classrooms were made available by better scheduling, the reassignment of space failed to answer the related problems. In many cases, classrooms or labs were not suitable for multi-use; in other cases, such as the cafeteria, the student union, the Beaton Institute and the Art Gallery, quarters were simply too small or outdated and more space was needed.

A year was lost in the meantime, but even as the ill-fated plan for the AVTC merger was underway, Scott was in communication with the local MP, federal minister and UCCB graduate, David Dingwall, and local MLA and provincial minister, Bernard Boudreau, as well as with ACOA, for a sizeable expansion costing up to $17,600,000, which would add 12,000 square metres (129,000 square feet) to the campus facility. Dingwall in particular, who worked closely with Scott and the board, was largely responsible for bringing the project to fruition. Sod-turning took place for the new Student, Culture and Heritage Centre December 10, 1994, a chilly, rainy, windy day, but applause was warm when Boudreau proclaimed that along with coal and steel, "UCCB is a pillar of Cape Breton."[82]

Unlike most North American universities, local architect, Spiro Trifos, had based the expansion on a European design linking all units together surrounding a central courtyard, featuring lawns, landscaping and seating areas. The red brick structure with a very textural design was elegant, dignified, yet innovative, with a plenty of glass, and with more traditional architectural features like balconies and an arched walkway. The building was officially opened September 6, 1997, to welcome an awed public to the huge Great Hall lined with artist Lewis Parker's murals portraying events in Cape Breton history, and a public display of a $1.4 million Picasso sketchbook, newly donated to the fine new Art Gallery. Under blue skies, local performers led a giant ceilidh in the new courtyard. Scott later claimed that she felt her two fondest achievements as president were a decent-looking campus and the new Art Gallery.[83] In the latter she was supported by Joe Shannon, who donated to it handsomely, and especially by Reuben Abramowsky, a wealthy Cape Breton-born Montreal clothier.

The expansion contained, besides the Art Gallery, new classrooms, a Students' Union centre, a multi-purpose hospitality area, the Beaton Institute archives, and administrative offices. It raised internal morale, not only in terms of giving more living space, but psychologically as well, in that the place finally looked like a campus; it was no longer the "high school on the highway," as it was sometimes called by its detractors. With the MacDonald Residence, improved landscaping, and well-maintained grounds, the campus was one that Cape Bretoners saw as the achievement of an old goal. As President Scott proclaimed, "The community dream is now a reality."[84] It was also during this time that the University College extended its ownership of lands adjoining the campus providing space for future expansion.[85]

Signs of the University College's coming of age were apparent not only in its physical expansion, but in its research capacity and concomitant role in community development. The Memorandum of Understanding (MOU) between the institution and ECBC continued to have a profound effect on the University College and the entire community throughout the 1990s. The SSHRC/NSERC Chair in the Management of Technological Change, together with ECBC and the Department of Research and Development, developed a strategy of plugging the community into the latest technological developments of the period, particularly in the rapidly growing field of information technology. Paul Patterson, who occupied the Chair, together with ECBC, encouraged the establishment of high-tech companies, whose representatives along with numerous community members, attended monthly meetings of a Technology Advisory Group (TAG) to exchange ideas and meet advocates and experts in technological entrepreneurship. Meetings were well attended and even televised. By 1993 more than 70 projects had received funding through the MOU, with emphasis on technological development, youth entrepreneurship, and graduate liaison programs with other universities. The program was unique in Canada in that government, the University College, and the community were working together for the economic transformation of a community.[86]

The MOU was responsible for numerous university research projects which affected the community. The computer assisted design and manufacturing facility (CAD/CAM) at the University College received extra funding to increase its prototyping and design modulating facilities, which in turn attracted advanced manufacturing companies to the job-starved community.[87] By 1994, Craig MacMullin now in charge of the Environmental Services Lab, with aid from the MOU, with strict management, and aggressive promotion, was able to capture 80 percent of environmental testing east of New Glasgow. The Lab employed 14 people and generated $500,000 in business that year alone.[88] Other labs followed: in virtual reality, geographic information system and global satellite positioning (GIS/GPS), and numerous smaller projects which became the showcase of UCCB's role in community research development.

It was obvious that the University College could act as a magnet to draw creative high-tech companies to the region through its unique academic and technology partnership. With that in mind plans were developed for a Technology Enterprise Centre on campus, a sort of incubator mall for newly developing high-tech companies. With the aid of the Canada/Nova Scotia Cooperative Agreement on Economic Development, and after much convincing of provincial bureaucrats, the sod for the Centre was turned by Federal Minister of Industry, John Manley, in November 1997. The Centre was designed to house 15 firms and was soon filled, not only with high-tech firms, but with a virtual firm representing new concepts in business education.[89] Many of the enterprises in the Centre eventually "graduated" into offices in the community.

The information technology initiatives led to the National Research Council's interest in locating a wireless technology lab on campus, which eventually occupied the entire Centre and promised to make Cape Breton a focus in the development of new communications technology.[90]

Besides information technology, petroleum development potential in the region also benefited from the University College's attention. In 1999, a Centre of Excellence in Petroleum Development and Petroleum Education was inaugurated to end the critical shortage of Atlantic Canadians in the knowledge of offshore gas development and production. The Centre attracted not only Canadians, but people from as far away as Angola, and received funding from Mobile Oil, Shell Canada and Westcoast Energy Limited.[91]

The success of the technology-oriented centres spurred on the development of academic alliances. Besides the well-established university-funded institutes, such as the Beaton and the Centre for International Studies, individual researchers were encouraged to open centres with internal and external linkages based on external funding. As a result over 15 new research centres were opened, including the Children's Rights Centre, which was established in 1995 and produced Canada's first children's rights curriculum for schools.[92] A Cape Breton Wellness Centre, a Centre for Housing Initiatives, a Centre for Humanomics, a Centre for Natural History, a Marketing Research Centre, a Multimedia Education Centre, a Community Economic Development Institute and a multi-faith Abraham Centre for Religion and Society were among the many others created. The Department of Research and Development's responsibilities had grown to the extent that, with its director's retirement, its work was divided between the academically-orientated Department of Research and Library Services and the Department of Economic and Technological Innovation.[93]

The interaction of the University College and the community was found not only in research and community-oriented centres, but was perhaps most obvious in the training of students for roles in the rapidly changing Cape Breton community. The Career Education Placement Centre, which was inaugurated to develop placement opportunities for students in work experience programs was placing more than 1,000 students annually by 1999.[94]

The delivery of these new programs rested largely on the financial ability of the University College to deliver them. Scott had inherited a financial situation which, though serious, was on the mend. At the beginning of her term in January 1993, most departments had control of their finances; pensions for retired administrators, such as Peter Hill and Tom MacNeil were easily covered thanks to lower interest payments on the declining debt. By Spring, ancillary services such as the Environmental Services Lab and the Book Store were making money and others saw their debts lowering. Still, 87.5 percent of the students, by far the highest rate in Nova Scotia, were studying on loans and student accounts receivable were up by $278,000. Without confirmation of loans and payment of these debts, the University College would suffer a revenue loss.[95]

Another threat to financial security was the end of the provincial government's wage freeze for publicly paid employees at the same time it continued to make cuts in its annual grants to universities. This was particularly harmful to UCCB, since its per capita grant per student was $1,700 less than the provincial average.[96] Without the help of the federal government, much needed repairs to the outdated boiler and heat pumps, the roof of the "A Wing" and other parts of the original structure dating from the 1960's, could not have been carried out.[97]

Funding pressures convinced the Board that the deficit would have to be retired in seven, rather than the planned five years.[98] As well, a program of early retirement packages and non-replacement of some positions was inaugurated. There were 21 early retirements with six non-replacements by June 1995.[99] It was by these means, as well as a rise in tuition and an extra $100,000 in the provincial grant that the 1995 budget was met.[100]

Scott tried to draw attention to the combined funding "crisis" situation of the institution when compared to its mainland competitors. She went so far as to observe the resentment as to the very nature of the University

College among her mainland colleagues. She pointed out that the University College was "out of the loop," due partly to its remote location, which did not lend itself to frequent meetings or social functions with the power brokers in the Halifax region, where the majority of the province's universities were located. "So, who we are and where we are [,] are two things working against us."[101] Necessary travel to Halifax alone cost the University College a "couple hundred thousand dollars" per year, a great deal more than the others who were near or in the capital. Distance made lobbying particularly difficult when it came to trying to convince politicians and bureaucrats to change the funding formula in recognition of the unusual character of the institution, with its relatively higher number of more costly programs in technology, engineering and science.[102]

Such pleas fell on deaf ears. Tuition had to rise by seven percent in 1996-97 when the province threatened a similar reduction in the operating grant.[103] The annual delay in funding announcements caused great concern to the institution's budget committee, and made planning almost impossible. The success of the University College's strict attention to spending, a 48-percent increase in tuition between 1991 and 1996, and non-replacement of staff and materials, resulted in small budget surpluses in the last four years of the 1990s.[104] All of this scrimping led to the University College's having the lowest operating budget ($3,679 per student) of any Canadian university. Scott, with the support of a petition signed by 1,500 students, lobbied the Nova Scotia Council for Higher Education for more funding. Though this occurred just at the time when that body was trying to pare down university budgets, she managed to get the province to recognize the need to develop the institution's highly regarded information technology programs. In April 1998, $1,000,000 was announced for two such centres of excellence in the province, one of which was at UCCB.[105]

This, however, did little to stop the mounting operating costs. The financial stress on the Board was shown when it rejected the proposed budgets for 1998-99, one with another 7.5 percent tuition increase, or an alternate one with a 2.5 percent increase, but a $1,456,117 deficit.[106] Consequently, the institution operated without a budget until June when a three-percent tuition increase and a $1,600,000 deficit was adopted.[107] This sort of situation was being repeated all over the province, and forced the government to increase its university operating grants by $24,000,000, giving UCCB $2,900,000 extra. The formula upon which this was based still failed to recognize the University College's isolation or program uniqueness, so still it did not gain as much money as other institutions of similar size.[108]

The funding was welcome, of course, and helped to offset a decrease of one percent in enrolment in 1999. It also meant tuition was raised by "only" 4.5-percent the following year. Even more important, the government announced a three percent reduction in provincial salaries, which allowed the University College to avoid a deficit, while placing a heavy strain on the morale of faculty and staff.[109] The faculty unions had decided in 1993 to reject the Shaw-Downey recommendation of the amalgamation of the academic and technology staff into one union, despite the fact that separate faculties had been abolished.[110] Scott was very much in favour of a single union, which she felt was more consistent with the unified model of learning the University College represented.[111] The unions bitterly opposed this, claiming that unification would add to morale problems and break a tradition which had existed since 1975.[112]

Relations between Scott and the unions remained cool, due partly to differing views on university governance, particularly noticeable in the role of deans. While deans were both academic and administrative officers, Scott saw them primarily as administrators, ensuring proper budget procedures and fair course allotments, but also working with fellow administrators for the common good of the institution. In this, the University College would differ from other universities where a much smaller decision-making body made decisions while deans represented the interests of their individual constituencies—often in competition with other deans. Many of the academic faculty, who had graduated from standard universities, favoured this latter model. Indeed, when, in 1998, Scott tried to enforce a policy of having deans sign an undated letter of resignation to be used in the event they could not agree with overall administrative policies, the head of the academic union, Michael Manson, stated bluntly "Deans are senior academic officials," and that their academic freedom must be protected.[113]

Scott says she had misgivings about taking a second term as president. As she later mused, she was both a hatchet person, there to end the chaos that had prevailed before her arrival, and a leader, there to put the place on the road. She worried that in the former role she had made too many enemies. She had the strong support of the Board chairman, Joe MacMullin, however, and he in turn had the support of the Board, so she accepted a second term, though she wondered privately if she would get to finish it. She was particularly interested in strengthening programs which would require faculty renewal by infusing new blood into in the institution which meant she would need faculty co-operation.[114] The differing philosophies and general coolness between Scott and the academic Faculty Association of University Teachers (FAUT) in particular set the stage for the University College's first collective agreement discussions. To that date the University College and the unions had merely a letter of understanding as to mutual obligations. However, the letter failed to mention how disputes should be settled.[115]

It was in this atmosphere that collective bargaining began in December 1999. The Canadian Union of Public Employees (CUPE), representing much of the non-teaching staff, decided to take a strike vote.[116] The NSGEU, representing technology and trades teachers, began bargaining at the same time, but the University College soon complained they were not bargaining in good faith. FAUT's negotiations were no more successful and both parties quickly applied for conciliation services.[117] Within a few weeks, members of both teaching unions had given their leaders a strike mandate, though further talks were still scheduled. The 65 CUPE employees who had been without a contract since 1997, voted in favour of a strike the following day.[118]

The only hope for reconciliation evaporated when, after one day of further conciliation, talks failed. A mandatory "cooling off" period followed, but the strike was set for January 14, 2000. Manson rallied the faculty stating that "the primary item is money and we are raring to go." He alleged that, though this was his union's first contract after the nine-year wage freeze, UCCB lagged behind most other universities who were already preparing for their second contract. "The university has the money and it is simply a question [of] where they want to spend it," Manson said.[119]

CUPE representatives meanwhile accepted the University College's contract proposal, while NSGEU bargaining was still underway, though 91 percent of its members had voted in favour of a strike.[120] Meanwhile, bargaining with FAUT grew more antagonistic. In an attempt to gain public sympathy in an area of declining employment, layoffs, and low wages, both sides went to the press with full-page ads carrying claims and counter claims of "unrealistic demands," the threat of rising tuition on one hand or the loss of staff due to low wages on the other.[121] The Nova Scotia Labour Relations Board found FAUT to be bargaining in bad faith in reintroducing its original wage offer during conciliation talks, a decision that only embittered talks all the more.[122] By early February talks broke down and a strike was called for February 11; the academic faculty hit the picket lines in temperatures as low as minus 23 degrees. At the same time, NSGEU went into two days of conciliation on February 4, but, within a week, accepted the University College's offer, having conceded nothing.[123]

However, FAUT faculty remained on the picket line. On February 22, negotiations began again, but broke down five days later with both sides still using the press to gain public support.[124] Students saw their term slipping away, and staged a small protest parade on Sydney's boardwalk.[125] More ominously perhaps, members from other militant unions joined the picket line, blocking the entrances to the Nova Scotia Community College, a call centre, located there, as well as students and staff of the University College. The RCMP turned back traffic until the pickets were withdrawn from the entrance.[126]

Peace and civility were elusive, and the viciousness grew. Insults flew and both sides launched defamation lawsuits. Scott was maligned and was targeted by hate mail.[127] In turn, administration angered faculty with paid advertisements meant to discredit. One such ad stated that faculty only taught nine hours per week for twenty-six weeks, implying this was the sum total of their employment responsibilities.[128] Lost teaching days were mounting, but renewed bargaining again failed, though many non-monetary issues were settled. On March 11, hope finally rose when the Minister of Labour appointed a mediator.[129] Within a week it seemed that all issues had been settled save the president's powers of layoff and termination of contract. When it was pointed out that presidents at other Atlantic universities had this power, the union seemed to accept the situation.[130]

On March 18, 75 percent of the voting academic staff agreed to accept its first collective agreement. It included a 20-percent wage increase over four years with a $3,500 signing bonus.[131] Defamation suits were also terminated after union president, Manson, and the FAUT leaders agreed to sign an apology to be published in the *Cape Breton Post*.[132] The University College in turn agreed to drop a later unfair bargaining complaint against the union. Seven teaching days were added to the class schedule to make up for lost class time.[133]

The strike was over, but its effects were long-lasting, not only in the interpersonal relations between the faculty and administration, and Scott in particular, but also in the University College's financial position. At budget talks the following June, students, who had largely supported their teachers' wage demands, walked out when a tuition increase of $500, or 14 percent, was proposed. This situation arose not only because of the wage increases, but because the government had withdrawn $1,500,000 from Trades training. "We are not in a position to generate the same revenues as other universities," claimed the University College's information officer, Suzanne Spencer.[134] A tuition increase of 10 percent was finally adopted, putting annual tuition at $4,000 for full-time students.[135]

Morale was also hit by the annual ranking of Canadian universities by *Maclean's* magazine. The unique nature of UCCB, its wide accessibility to students, and its low level of funding kept UCCB near the bottom of the rankings, though it placed high in the "value-added" category and personal attention given to students.[136] The low ranking continued during the 90s and, though Scott rightfully declared, and *Maclean's* agreed, that the survey "is not terribly meaningful to us," it did affect morale of the very dedicated staff. The lack of money available for scholarships and bursaries, was another cause of the University College's slipping to last place in the ranking of small universities in Canada, even though it placed highly in areas over which it had some control, such as research funding.[137]

The bitter legacy of the strike and the backlash from low ratings influenced the life of the University College in the early years of the new millennium. These elements became particularly telling during the budget discussions. The first budget after the strike was accepted though students had staged a walkout at discussions.[138] An atmosphere of rancour prevailed during the entire process, and students and faculty representatives questioned its validity. Scott and the administration, in line with her determination to maintain the viability of the institution by keeping it out of debt, were firm in seeking to clean out under-subscribed courses. The Budget Committee was raising serious concerns as to the sustainability of courses which, while intrinsically valuable, had low enrolment. The diploma in Office Administration was suspended on these grounds.[139]

The following year, a proposed six-percent tuition increase, together with layoffs, was strongly opposed by student and faculty representatives.[140] The University College's Chief Financial Officer, Gordon MacInnis, claimed that the province had failed to live up to its financial commitments for 2000-2001, so the University College had been forced to adopt an early-retirement incentive plan supported by a long-term transitional fund which would eventually allow long-term savings.[141] By tight budgeting and project-based external funding he felt the institution could come in with a half-million dollar budget surplus for 2001.[142]

However, in September, Scott and the Board, in the name of long-term savings, ordered course cuts in some low-enrolment courses. Academic Council, composed heavily of teaching faculty, strongly resented what they saw as Scott's heavy-handed refusal to take Council's advice and role in bicameral governance. A new Board was not as supportive of Scott as previous ones. Faculty members on the board questioned the role of Academic Council *vis-à-vis* the president, and felt the course cancellations to be "a little impulsive," pointing to the anxiety they were causing faculty and students. The old question of the Board's role in management came up yet again, raising questions dating back to William Reid's tenure. The Board supported Scott's position that the Academic Council was advisory to the president and that the course cuts had to be made.[143] As a result, 24 courses or sections of courses were cut. Scott reiterated that the University College must address the problem of class sizes of less than six students since the institution was underfunded and could no longer sustain them. Unfortunately, many of these classes were third- and fourth-year level courses, which affected potential graduates.[144]

The ill feeling that many of the more vocal members of faculty expressed toward Scott spilled into the budget talks the following year. At open sessions of the Board on the budget the issue of course cancellations, the role of Academic Council in the budget process, and UCCB's mission all came to the fore. The first overcrowded session attracted so many faculty members that it was moved to larger quarters in the Boardmore Playhouse, a fitting scene for the unfolding drama.[145] The bitterness, as usual, found its way to the press. Michael MacSween, president of the Students' Union, claimed that the University College was mismanaged: "It's a sickness that this university faces and it's coming from the top."[146] The *Cape Breton Post* even reported that the Students' Union had proposed an alternate budget which it presented behind closed doors to some interested Board members.[147] If this was the case, the support of the Board for Scott must have been in question. As well, a number of technology, Trades and business instructors published an ad declaring the budgetary process "flawed," and alleging that insufficient money was going into the classroom. They sought "alternate solutions" to Scott's course cuts.[148] Scott replied, "Our look at the information has been exhaustive over the last several months," and that the cost-cutting moves were necessary. She went further to say that certain members of the Budget Committee "have a particular political agenda, and they will feel that way [opposed to her changes] regardless of what information is given them."[149]

Scott failed to gain full support from the Board and the proposed budget was tabled.[150] A further overcrowded public budget session of the Board was held in April, but those present refused to move to larger quarters and the session was continually disrupted, though further attacks on the budget by some faculty were finally heard. Scott defended the budget on the grounds that the longer the Board delayed in making changes—both cuts and investments in new courses—the more precarious would be the financial and intellectual base of the institution. The budget, however, was defeated by a vote of thirteen to fifteen.[151] The following month, a second revised budget was, by a vote of eighteen to eight, approved.[152] By that time, Jacquelyn Scott had submitted her resignation.

Gordon MacInnis became Chief Administrative Officer and as such reported directly to the Board at its meeting in June 2002. A new president, John Harker, was appointed June 26, 2003, beginning a new chapter in a remarkable story.

Fig. 10. Aerial Overviews / G. Langille. Aerial view of UCCB campus, 2002. Courtesy UCCB.

Epilogue

The dream of a centre of higher education in Cape Breton was an old one that became a reality through the focus and the labour of many people. It has never been a simple dream, for it envisions a new kind of institution, one reflecting its community—a blend of industry with a deep vein of creativity and admiration for intellectual, as well as practical, achievement. Accordingly, its community values it highly.

Yet there is still much to achieve, with respect to the vision set out for it, and the reasons for that are many. Enmity of rival institutions, under-funding, a shaky local economy, provincial governments that have never really recognized the uniqueness of the institution, its role in the economy, or its consequent special needs.

Internally, the dual nature of the institution and its community role have never been accepted by many faculty. Its location makes it seem remote to many people in Cape Breton, who subsequently lack a sense of ownership for the institution.

Unlike the other universities in Nova Scotia, UCCB is a product of the mid-twentieth century, a time when religious influences were waning, when education was becoming available to the average person, and becoming the norm rather than the exception. In addition, universities were being called upon to be centres of economic development. UCCB, partly because of its activist roots, partly because of the needs of its community stepped rather easily into this role. The innovative nature of the university provided fertile ground for imaginative programs that placed it well in front of its mainland rivals. The difficulty was that, despite its singular ability to respond to the changing role of higher education—in fact to do what universities were being asked to do—financing could never keep up with the demands that were being placed upon the institution. Given its rapid development and low funding, various administrations have followed the same pattern: a burst of creativity, a flood of new programs, followed by the realization of under-funding, then budget shortfalls, attempted restraints, recriminations, and resignations.

The whole situation has been made worse by the economic and population decline of Cape Breton Island. As a result, the university has been called upon to aid in the economic development of the area and with government assistance has done so. Yet the provincial government has been restricted in its ability to help by the justifiable needs of more "senior" universities. Without the help of the federal government, many of the economic benefits the university has brought to Cape Breton would not have been possible. Yet provincial funding is still a problem every administration has to face. Until this is settled, the university is saddled with the same cycle of hope and disappointment.

Despite this, the University College has made immeasurable achievements: it has turned out successful graduates in all walks of life, it has helped reinvigorate the economy and spirit of its community—indeed it is impossible to imagine the Island without UCCB. It seems an almost inexhaustible source of assistance to every phase of life: its staff, institutes, arts centres, sports teams, community access programs, its contacts with outside institutions, communities, and other countries, bring immeasurable benefits to Cape Breton. The challenge is to continue the amazing creativity that has characterized the first half-century of the institution.

From what has gone before, one cannot help but believe that the university college will devise exciting new approaches toward education and community development, and even novel configurations of its own structure. UCCB has not remained static, it has charted new paths *because* of the obstacles it faced. Resistance and determination have been the catalysts for its creativity, an imaginative approach that is part of its very fiber.

Obstacles will come and go, but if past history is any indication, if all these threads can be brought together in a unified vision during the next half-century, the obstacles even partly overcome, they will strengthen the institution and Canada will have a great deal to be proud of in its first university college.

Fig. 11 Reverend Dr. Malcolm A. MacLellan

Fig. 12 Rev. Dr. Donald F. Campbell

Fig. 13 Mr. John Terry

Fig. 14 Dr. William Reid

Fig. 15 Dr. Peter Hill

Fig. 16 William Gallivan

Fig. 17 Dr. Jacquelyn Thayer Scott, O.C.

Fig. 18 H. John Harker. LLD

NOTES

Chapter One

1. A.A. Johnston, *History of the Catholic Church in Eastern Nova Scotia*, 479-481.
2. Ibid vol. I and II, 89, 156, 158. Arichat Academy was established in 1833.
3. Ibid vol. II 299, 300; vol. I, 92-93.
4. Ibid vol. II, 310-311.
5. Donovan, "May Learning Flourish," 105.
6. *Post*, 2 September 1905.
7. *Post*, 20 September 1922.
8. *Post*, 20 October 1931.
9. *Post*, 27 April 1937.
10. Cameron, *For The People*, 213.
11. D.S. Morrison to George Morrison, 27 March 1938, D.S. Morrison Papers.
12. Ibid.
13. Ibid.
14. Ibid.
15. Thomas O'Reilly Boyle (1896-1966) was a native of Placentia, Newfoundland, but moved at an early age to Whitney Pier, Sydney. He was ordained to the Catholic priesthood in 1921, and served in parishes in Cape Breton and later in Toronto and Michigan. He taught in the People's School 1921-1922 and in 1961 published *Justice Through Power*, a labour study. He associated with J. B. McLachlan, a far-seeing, though left-leaning labour leader. Some of his papers are found in the Beaton Institute. See also Cameron, *For the People* 198 and fn. 15, 476-477.
16. Coady was also Rev. Jimmy Tompkins' double first cousin. They had grown up together in Margaree, Cape Breton.
17. Ibid, 212-246.
18. Ibid, 246.
19. Ibid, 266-272.
20. Ibid, 283.
21. Ibid, 254.
22. *Post*, 23 September 1947.
23. As the completion of Grade 11 was sufficient for entry into Nova Scotia universities at the time, students who had Grade 11 would spend two years at the college. Those with Grade 12 would spend only one year (sophomore) there before continuing elsewhere.
24. *Post*, 23 September 1947.
25. Nearing, *He Loved the Church*, 118.
26. Nearing, 101.
27. MacLellan, *Xavier Junior College*, 2-4.
28. Nearing, 107.
29. MacLellan, *Xavier Junior College*, 3.
30. Hugh J. Somers, son of an Antigonish merchant and alumnus of St. FX, had served as university treasurer. A long-time friend of Bishop MacDonald, he was vice-president (1944-1954), and later president (1954-1964).
31. MacLellan, *Xavier Junior College*, 3-5.
32. Ibid, 5. There is no record of an official discussion with University faculty.

33. The Board was represented by Rev. Leo B. Sears, A.A. MacIntyre, and Colin Mackenzie. The University Council appointed Dr. MacLellan, H.J. Somers and Rev. Allan I. MacAdam.
34. Lyceum Restoration, nd, BI; Reports: Museums, 3-5.
35. MacLellan, *Xavier Junior College*, 7-8.
36. Ibid, 9.
37. Ibid.
38. Ibid, 9-10.
39. Ibid, 11.
40. Ibid, 12.
41. Ibid, 13.
42. Ibid.
43. *Post*, 7 March 1951.
44. MacLellan, *Xavier Junior College*, 15.
45. Journal of M.A. MacLellan, 10-20 March 1951, BI, MG 13, 59.
46. MacLellan, *Xavier Junior College*, 14.
47. Ibid, 20.
48. Father "Charlie" was known as, "little" Charlie to folks around his home environs; "beag" in the Gaelic.
49. MacLellan, *Xavier Junior College*, 21-22.
50. Of the three Navy League Huts constructed, one had been burned by the arsonist in March, the second was later used by St George's Parish as a hall, and the College was born in the third.
51. MacLellan, *Xavier Junior College*, 25.
52. MacLellan, *Xavier Junior College*, 32.
53. *Post*, 16 January 1952.
54. *Post*, 17 January 1952.
55. M. M. Coady to M. A. MacLellan, telegram, 16 January 1952. BI, Scrap Book 1, "Xavier College, 1951-1960," 20.

Chapter Two

1. M.A. MacLellan, *The Importance of Conservatism In Education*, 44.
2. Ibid, 36.
3. Ibid,16, 45.
4. MacLellan, *Xavier Junior College*, 36.
5. Ibid, 40-41.
6. Ibid, 41.
7. Ibid, 55.
8. The Board's original members were Rev. A.A. Beaton, Ben O'Neil, Alfred Reynolds of Sydney, Perry Cadigan of Glace Bay, Stephen Dolhanty of Florence, Syd Oram of Sydney Mines, M.R. Campbell, Assistant General Superintendent of Dominion Iron and Steel, G.G. Campbell Principal of Sydney Academy, Alvin Holmes, Councillor and Co-op leader in New Waterford, and Charles Miller.
9. Ibid, 45-46.
10. Ibid, 51-52.
11. Ibid, 52.
12. Ibid, 37. The chief early benefactors of the library were Monsignor MacGillivray and Rev. Michael MacCormack of East Bay.
13. The price paid was $40,000. MacLellan, *Xavier Junior College*, 58.

14. Ibid, 47.
15. Ibid, 48-49.
16. St. FX Board of Governors, "Interim Report Of The Joint Committee of Governors and Faculty In Regard To University Expansion," (20 December 1955. BI. MG1,1,A2, Box 1, File 7).
17. Ibid.
18. Ibid.
19. Scrap Book, *Xavier College*, 1951-1960, 80.
20. Ibid., 131.
21. Ibid.
22. Scrap Book, *Xavier College*, 1960-1964, 66.
23. *Facts About Xavier* [1964], BI, MG 1,1, A2a, file 18.
24. St. Francis Xavier University, Committee on Enrolment and Expansion, 4 April 1964, MG 1, 1, A2, file 6.
25. *Facts about Xavier.*
26. Annual Bulletin, Xavier College, 1960-1961; Xavier College, General Information [1963-1964], 36; Scrap Book, *Xavier College*, 1960-1964, 136.
27. Ibid., 82; *Chronicle Herald*, 6 December 1962.
28. Ibid., 125.
29. Scrap Book, *Xavier Junior College*, 1951-1964, 133.
30. St. FX Board of Governors, 13 May 1958, MG 1,1, A2, box 2, file 7. The Standard Brands Building was located on the site of the later Science Building.
31. St. FX Board of Governors, 26 October 1959; H.J. Somers, Report for the Academic year 1959-1960, 2 September 1960, both in MG 1,1, A2, box 2, file 7.
32. St. FX Board of Governors, 13 May 1958, MG 1,1, A2, box 2, file 7.
33. M.R. Chappell was the general contractor for the building.
34. St. FX Board of Governors, 20 October 1958, Scrap Book 1, 133. The Logue property was purchased for $40,000. MacLellan, *Xavier Junior College*, 58.
35. The building's commemorative plaque is now located in the Beaton Institute.
36. *Post*, 20 September 1960.
37. St. FX Board of Governors, 20 September 1960, H.J. Somers, Report, Academic Year 1959-1960. MG 1,1,A2, box 1, file 7.
38. John J. Nicholson, *St. FX Has a Soul,* [c.1971], MG 1,1, A13, file 1a.
39. Report of the Committee on Enrolment (sic), [1963], MG 1,1,A2a, file 6, pp.2-3.
40. Ibid, 3.
41. Ibid, 2.
42. Meeting of the Committee on Enrolment and Expansion, 27 February 1964, MG 1,1,A2a, file 6. The author, who was on staff at the time, was aware of the problem.
43. St. FX Board of Governors, 18 October 1961, MG 1,1,A2, box 1, file 7.
44. Minutes, Committee on Enrolment and Expansion, 22 February 1964, MG 1,1, A2a, file 6. Xavier representatives on the Committee were William Reid, Owen Carrigan, Rev. Gregory MacLeod, and Dr. MacLellan.
45. At the next meeting of the committee this proposed name was changed to St. FX University of Sydney. Minutes, Committee on Enrolment and Expansion, 14 March 1964.
46. Minutes of the Committee on Enrolment and Expansion, 22 February 1964.
47. Minutes of the Committee on Enrolment and Expansion, 14 March 1964.
48. MacLellan, *Xavier Junior College*, 55-56.
49. Minutes of the Committee on Enrolment and Expansion, 14 March 1964.
50. Ibid.
51. Ibid.
52. MacLellan, *Xavier Junior College*, 57.

53. MacLellan, *Xavier Junior College*, 60-62.
54. Xavier Junior College was renamed Xavier College in 1963.
55. MacLellan, *Xavier Junior College*, 63.
56. Ibid.

Chapter Three

1. Campbell was the son of Judge A. D. "Hump" Campbell and Pearl Currie of Sydney. He was a graduate of Sydney Academy.
2. Charles W. MacDonald (1916-1973), a native of Inverness, was the son of John Roderick MacDonald and Maria MacLeod and a graduate of St. FX. He completed his studies at La Grande Seminaire in Montreal and was ordained in 1942. He performed parish duties in the Diocese of Antigonish and was appointed Professor of Philosophy at Xavier in 1951, receiving his PhD from the University of Ottawa in 1964, while serving as director of Athletics at St. FX.
3. D.F. Campbell, *What's In a Name?,* Appendix C, Reports: Education, B.I.; St Francis Xavier University, Minutes of Senate, 19 October 1972, "Full-time Student Registration," MG 1, 1 A1, file 90.
4. Minutes of the Committee of Enrolment and Expansion, 4 April 1964, MG1,1,A2a, file 6.
5. These properties included Quinan Hall, a recreational centre owned by Sacred Heart Parish and the Standard Foods Building. Xavier Clippings, Scrap Book 2, 1960-64, 125.
6. Press Release, 19 October 1964, MG 1, 1, A2a, file 18.
7. Press Release, 20 October 1964, ibid.
8. *Post*, 17 November 1964.
9. Campbell, 4.
10. Ibid., 4-5; *Post*, 6 September 1966. Maritime builders were the general contractors for the building.
11. Xavier College Scrapbook 4, 31. The Extension Department, which had been occupying one of the buildings demolished for the science building, moved to 26 Nepean Street temporarily and then to 116 George Street in the fall of 1965. *Post*, 12 August 1965.
12. *Xcalibur*, 26 November 1965; *Chronicle Herald*, 4 January 1966.
13. Campbell, 5.
14. *Report of the Senate Sub-Committee on Xavier-St. FX Relations*, 18 March 1972, MG 1,1, A2a, file1,h.
15. Taylor, Leiberfeld and Heldman, *A Physical Plant Development Program for Xavier College*, March, 1967, 151ff, MG 1,1, A2a, file 2a.
16. Ibid., 161.
17. *Ibid.*, 179.
18 *Summary of Faculty Opinions From A Circulated Questionnaire*, enclosure in William Reid to D.F. Campbell, 11 August 1967, MG 1, 1,A2a, file2a.
19. "Xavier to Become a Full University," *Xavier Scrapbook* 4, 150; *Post*, 11 August, 15 September 1966.
20. "Kaper Korner" in the *Spokesman*, vol. 1, #3, [Fall, 1966].
21. *Xaverian Weekly*, 7 October 1966.
22. *Post*, 5 December 1966; *The Casket*, 8 December 1966.
23. Sister Margaret Harquail, Congregation of Notre Dame, was the first full-time appointment.
24. Campbell, 6.; Xavier Scrapbook 4, 261.
25. *Post*, 27 October 1967.
26. *Post*, 6 November 1967.

27. Taylor, Leiberfeld and Heldman (Canada), *Report to St. Francis Xavier University, An Analysis of Prospective Growth and Development Patterns*, January, 1969, Chapter Two.
28. Ibid., 6.
29. Ibid., 91-93.
30. Members from the St. FX campus were Rev. Gregory MacKinnon (later president of the University), Rev. Murdoch MacLean, and John J. Sears. Xavier representatives were Rev. C.W. MacDonald, William Reid, and Dr. D. F. Campbell.
31. Three members of a six member committee to study the Second Leiberfeld Report to the University Council, St Francis Xavier University, n.d, 7.
32. Ibid., 8-9.
33. Report of the Committee Members From Xavier College, attached in D.F. Campbell, Report of the Council Subcommittee on the Second Leiberfeld Report, n.d. The two-year program was again endorsed at the Board meeting of 17 January 1969. Board of Governors, 17 January 1969, MG1, 1, A1, file 35.
34. Campbell, 7.
35. Ibid.
36. *Post*, 30 January 1970.
37. *Submission to the Board of Governors of Saint Francis Xavier University On Xavier College Development From Xavier College Faculty*, December, 1968.
38. Allan J. MacEachen (Minister of Health and Welfare) to M.A. MacLellan, 3 November 1967, MG 1,1, A2a, file 3; Board of Governors, St. FX, 15 May 1968, MG 1,1, A1, file 35; D. F. Campbell to M.A. MacLellan, 30 January 1968, MG 1,1, A1, file 35; A. J. MacEachen to M.A. MacLellan, 8 October 1968, MG 1,1, A2a, file 3).
39. *Post*, 12 October 1968.
40. Board of Governors, 17 January 1969, MG1, 1, A1, file 35.
41. Ibid.
42. Ibid.; *Post*, 23 January 1969, 17 February 1969.
43. Board of Governors, 6 May 1969, MG 1,1 A1, file 35.
44. *Post*, 12 May 1969.
45. Board of Governors, 17 April 1970, file 35.
46. Murphy to MacLellan, 4 June 1970, in Board of Governors, 19 June 1970, file 35.
47. Ibid.
48. *Post*, 30 September 1970.
49. Board of Governors, 29-30 October 1970, file 35.
50. Ibid.
51. *Post*, 31 October 1970.
52. *Xcalibur*, December, 1970.
53. *Highlander*, 9 December 1970; Xavier College, Meeting Regarding Xavier Expansion, 11 November 1970, MG 1, 1, A2a, file 1h.
54. Ibid.
55. Board of Governors, 6 February 1971, MG 1, A1, file 46.
56. Regan, Gerald, Speech at Sydney Forum, February 3, 1971. MG 9, 27, 7.
57. Ibid., 8.
58. Ibid.
59. *Highlander*, 10 February 1971.
60. *Chronicle Herald*, 7 April 1971.
61. Board of Governors, 30 April 1971, Appendix A, MG 1,1, A1, file 35. Campbell, 11.
62. Ibid.
63. Ibid., 6 May 1971, file 46.
64. *Post*, 4 April 1972.

65. Board of Governors, 22 October 1971, file 35. Campbell, 3.
66. *Highlander*, 6 November 1968.
67. Cunningham Interview.
68. Campbell, 3.
69. Campbell to All Faculty Members, Committee of Co-operation Between Xavier and Nova Scotia Eastern Institute of Technology, 8 November 1971, MG 1, 1, A2a, file 1, (1g2); Minutes, Meeting of the Joint Committee, Deans and Registrars of Xavier College and NSEIT. 8 November 1972.
70. Report of the Senate Subcommittee on Xavier-St. FX Relations, 18 March 1972.
71. Committee members were Donald Fewer (Chair), Douglas Campbell, John Nicholson, Michael MacDonald, Andrew Hogan and John J. MacDonald. The committee was appointed 4 October 1971.
72. Report of the Senate Subcommittee on Xavier-St. FX Relations, 18 March 1972, 8.
73. Ibid.
74. Ibid., 29-30.
75. Campbell, 15; *Post*, 13 April 1972. The vote was 25-16.
76. Campbell, 15.
77. *Post,* 14 April 1970.
78. *Post*, 15 May 1972.
79. The building was located on the corner of George and Pitt streets and was a former automobile showroom owned by R.J. Logue, an early patron of the College.
80. John. J. MacDonald, John T. Sears, J.T. Langley represented The main campus; Xavier representatives were Dr. D.F. Campbell, William Reid and Donald V. Fewer (Registrar).
81. Report of the Committee on Structures to the University Senate, 16 February 1973.
82. Campbell, 16. The committee was announced at St. FX, 19 February and the next day at Sydney.
83. Members of the Committee were D.F. Campbell, Tom Kent (DEVCO), Michael Kirby (government representative), J.J. MacDonald (St. FX), Rev. Malcolm MacDonnell (St. FX), Harold Mason, Hugh Somers (St. FX) and Arthur Murray, Chair (University Grants Committee).
84. Joseph A. Lauwreys, *Final Report*, 5.
85. Ibid.
86. Campbell, 17.
87. Ibid.
88. Lauwerys, 8.
89. This firm had previously totally planned Seneca College and had completed substantial work on universities at Toronto, Guelph, and Kingston Ontario.
90. Ibid., 18-19.
91. Recommendations of the Special Committee Appointed by Premier Regan to present a plan for Post-secondary Education in Cape Breton.
92. Supplementary Report of the Special Committee Appointed by Premier Regan to present a plan for Post-secondary Education in Cape Breton, 26 February 1973.
93. St. FX Board of Governors, 18 February 1973.
94. Lauwerys, 3.
95. St. FX Board of Governors, 18 February 1973.
96. Ibid.
97. Senate, 9, 16 April, 1973.
98. *Post*, 13 April 1973.
99. Ibid.
100. *Xaverian Weekly*, 29 March 1973. MacDonald died 26 March 1973.

101. *Post*, 18 April 1973.
102. *Post*, 22 April 1973.
103. *Post*, 11 May 1973.
104. *Chronicle Herald*, 11 May 1973.
105. Campbell, 20; *Chronicle Herald*, 11 May 1973.
106. *Post*, 17 July 1973. Thomas L. Sullivan was elected chair, succeeding Donald B. MacIsaac.
107. *Post*, 22 September 1973; Campbell, 20.
108. Members of this group included Campbell, Dr. Malcolm MacLellan, Edo Gatto (both of St. FX), Donald MacIsaac and Robert MacKenzie (Sydney residents), Gregory MacLeod and Robert Brisco (Xavier faculty), Brian Conrod and John Coleman (NSEIT faculty), Judith Rolls and Ignatius MacQueen (Xavier Student Union), Curtis MacNeil and Sheldon Hartling (NSEIT Student Union), Denne Burchell and John L. Dodge (DEVCO), J. Colin Campbell, Angus MacKillop, Allister MacLeod, Reva Nathanson, Rudy Pace, Jean MacFadgen, Arthur LeBlanc, and Clarence Nicholson (appointees from Cape Breton of the provincial government), Percy Fleet, G.R. MacLean, H.P. Timmons and H. F. MacRae (mainland appointees of the provincial government).

Chapter Four

1. Executive Committee, St. FX Board of Governors, 4 October 1973.
2. *Post*, 21 November 1973.
3. *Post*, 11 July 1973. "Little X" was a term used locally in reference to Xavier College.
4. Terry Interview.
5. Cunningham Interview.
6. Executive Committee, St. FX Board of Governors, 4 October 1973, 15 November 1973, 29 December 1973; Special Advisory Committee Minutes, 28 February 1974.
7. Executive Committee, St. FX Board of Governors, 4 October 1973; Special Advisory Committee Minutes, Minutes, 7 February 1974.
8. Minutes of the Advisory Committee, 8 February 1974.
9. *Chronicle-Herald*, 11 January 1974. Enrolment had declined 13 percent.
10. Minutes of the Executive Committee of the Advisory Committee, (the terms "board" and "committee" were used interchangeably) 7 February 1974; Minutes of the Advisory Committee, 8 February 1974. Other suggested names were Bourinot College, DesBarres Academy, Cabot College, C.W. MacDonald Memorial College, Bras d'Or College, Isle Royale Institute, Arteck University and Louisbourg University of Cape Breton. *Post,* 14 January 1974.
11. Other members of the committee were D.F. Campbell, Rev. Clarence Nicholson, Denne Burchell, Greg MacLeod, Arthur LeBlanc, Tom Jala (NSEIT), and Jean MacFadgen of Sydney. Advisory Committee, 23 May 1974.
12. Ibid., 17 June 1974.
13. Ibid.
14. Ibid.
15. *Chronicle-Herald*, 30 May, 5 June 1974.
16. Ibid. Most active in this regard were writer Eileen Henry and fellow councillor, Colin Chisholm.
17. Ibid., 25 June 1974.
18. Ibid.
19. Report of the President to the Board of Governors, College of Cape Breton (henceforth Board, unless otherwise indicated), 11 October 1974, in Minutes, Board of Governors, 24 July 1974.

20. Laws of Nova Scotia, 1974, Chapter 4, 23 Eliz. II, *An Act to Establish the College of Cape Breton.*
21. Lyndon MacIntyre, *Chronicle-Herald*, 7 June 1974.
22. Very Reverend Clarence Nicholson, DDiv., was formally elected 12 October 1973 as first chair of the board of the College of Cape Breton. He had been a member of the Advisory Committee since 1973, and at the time was minister at Carmen United Church, Sydney Mines. He was former Principal of Pine Hill Divinity College in Halifax and past Moderator of the United Church of Canada. He was appointed Officer of the Order of Canada in 1973. *Post*, 12 October 1974.
23. Report of the President to the Board of Governors, CCB (henceforth Board of Governors), 11 October 1947, in Minutes, Board of Governors, 25 July 1974.
24. Board of Governors, Annual General Meeting, 11 October 1974.
25. Board of Governors, 13 December 1974.
26. Included in this department were Rev. A.B. Campbell, Bursar, Mary Hines, Manager of Accounting and Garnet Ward, Manager of Purchasing.
27. *Post*, 11 July 1975.
28. Board of Governors, 21 January 1975.
29. Rudderham had held the position of Vice-Principal at NSEIT. George Brown became Coordinator, Trades Training, Vincent J. Cunningham, Coordinator of Engineering Technology, and William A. MacAulay, Coordinator of Business Technology.
30. Board of Governors, 11 March 1976.
31. Report of the President to the Board of Governors, 11 October 1974, in Minutes, Board of Governors, 25 July 1974. In visiting other campuses, they found no models that could help realize the vision of the new college.
32. College Council, 17 February 1983.
33. Cunningham. Members of the committee were Peter Dawson (then at Memorial University), Vince Cunningham, Bill MacAulay, Reid and Donald Dunbar.
34. Ibid.
35. Special Meeting, Board of Governors, 25 October 1974.
36. Board of Governors, 13 December 1974.
37. President's Report, 1974-1975, Board of Governors, 30 October 1975.
38. The proposed senate would be composed of 10 members from each faculty, 7 from administration, 6 students and 3 from the community.
39. Board of Governors, 29 October 1976, 11 March 1976. It was stressed at the time that the Council was to be a "creature of the Board of Governors" which could amend its by-laws without a two-thirds vote of Council.
40. College Council, 15 December 1976.
41. College Council, 21 February 1978, 20 September 1978.
42. College Council, 24 January 1980.
43. College Council, 26 April 1978, 25 May 1978.
44. The vote endorsing in principle the academic merit of the program was 11 for, 14 against with 5 abstentions. College Council, 31 March 1981.
45. Ibid.
46. Ibid., 26 June 1983.
47. Board of Governors, 30 October 1975.
48. College Council, 31 March 1981.
49. Board of Governors, 26 February 1982.
50. College Council, 15 June 1982.
51. *Post*, 12 September 1975.

52. Report of the President for 1974-75 to the Board of Governors, 30 October 1975.
53. Board of Governors, 29 October 1976.
54. *Post*, 19 August 1983. The Institute operated until 1989.
55. Pioneer members of the Beaton Institute included Yvonne Campbell, Kay MacDonald, Gaelic-speaking researcher and secretary, and Doug MacPhee, noted pianist and expert in Cape Breton's Scottish music.
56. Board of Governors, 30 October 1975, 25 November 1976.
57. MacLeod Interview. MacLeod was actively involved in the vision of the Institute.
58. *Post*, 17 April 1981.
59. College Council, 20 April 1983, 25 October 1983, 21 November 1983.
60. Report of the President 1974-75, Boards of Governors, 30 October 1975.
61. College Council, 25 May 1978.
62. Executive, Board of Governors, 14 December 1979.
63. Executive, Board of Governors and Board of Governors, 7 February 1980.
64. Executive, Board of Governors, 29 October 1981.
65. Board of Governors, 21 June 1982; College Council, 29 September 1982.
66. College Council, 30 September 1983, 21 November 1983, 1 March 1984.
67. Woodcock and Associates. *Master Plan.*
68. Advisory Committee, 2 May 1974.
69. St. FX Board of Governors, 14 July 1974, 3 October 1974.
70. William Gillis to Campbell, 4 September 1974, MG 1, 1, A2a, file 1, 1f 52.
71. Board of Governors, Report of the Campus Development Committee, 13 December 1974.
72. Board of Governors, Report of the Campus Development Committee, 13 December 1974; Executive Committee, Board of Governors, 21 January 1975.
73. Board of Governors, 18 February 1975; Executive Committee, Board of Governors, 21 February, 1 April 1975.
74. *Post*, 16 January 1975; Campbell to Arthur L. Murphy, 14 July 1975, in attachment, Board of Governors, 26 September 1975.
75. Campbell to Murphy, 24 January 1975, in attachment, Board of Governors.
76. *Post*, 20 August 1975.
77. Ibid., 25 August 1975.
78. Executive Committee, Board of Governors, 27 August 1975.
79. Board of Governors, 30 October 1975.
80. *Post*, 7 November 1975.
81. Ibid., 8 November 1975.
82. Campus Development Committee, Status Report, October, 1977, MG 1,1,A2a, F1,f51.
83. Ibid.
84. Ibid; also 17 April 1976.
85. Executive, Board of Governors, 21 July 1977.
86. Executive, Board of Governors, 23 September 1977.
87. Board of Governors, 28 October 1977.
88. Campbell to Wallace, 4 October 1977, MG 1,1, A2a, file 1, 1f51.
89. Executive, Board of Governors, 2 February 1978.
90. Executive, Board of Governors, 6 April 1978; Campus Development Committee, budget Forecast, 1 February 1978, MG 1, 1 A2a, file 1, 1f51.
91. Ibid.
92. Board of Governors, 7 April, 9 June 1978; Executive, Board of Governors, 27 April 1978.
93. Board of Governors, 9 April 1978.
94. Executive, Board of Governors, 11 June 1979.

95. Board of Governors, 24 October 1979.
96. Board of Governors. 25 April 1980.
97. Executive, Board of Governors, 31 July 1981.
98. Executive, Board of Governors, 29 October 1981; Board of Governors, 30 October 1981.
99. This amounted to $177,000 for the Project Officer and $77,000 for a health tax rebate. The college presumably paid the rest. Executive, Board of Governors, 28 October 1983.
100. Report of the President, Board of Governors, 11 October 1974, in Board of Governors, 25 July 1974.
101. *Post*, 30 August 1975.
102. Ibid., 26 September 1975; full time breakdown was Technology 614, Arts and Science 600.
103. Executive Committee, Board of Governors, 9 October 1975.
104. The breakdown in numbers: arts and science 601, technology 426, trades full time equivalent 185. Board of Governors, 29 October 1976.
105. Ibid., 17 December 1976. Fifty-nine percent of students in Cape Breton completed grade 12 versus the Canadian average of seventy percent, College Council, 30 January 1979.
106. Board of Governors, 27 May 1977.
107. Ibid., 26 October 1978.
108. Ibid., 24 October 1979, 24 October 1980.
109. Ibid., President's Report, 24 October 1980.
110. Ibid.
111. Executive, Board of Governors, 29 October 1981, College Council, 20 November 1981.
112. College Council, 26 April, 22 September 1982.
113. Ibid.; *Post*, 19 August 1983.
114. Board of Governors, 28 October 1983, 26 October 1984.
115. *Post*, 12 May 1975.
116. Board of Governors, 1 May 1975. Organizers were Brian Conrod and William Wiseman.
117. Board of Governors, 11 March 1976. It was agreed to register the logo and coat-of arms to avoid their misuse in 1977. Executive, Board of Governors, 27 October 1977.
118. Executive, Board of Governors, 10 March 1976; Board of Governors, 11 March 1976. Carl Buchanan was a member of the committee choosing the new colours. He favoured white and orange, the colours of his alma mater, the University of Tennessee. The green was added to indicate the rolling hills of Cape Breton, the orange for the institution's bright future and the white, the innocence of the new institution. Since that time 12 schools have adopted these colours in the U.S. and Canada. As for the name "Capers", other possibilities, such as "Highlanders" has been suggested, but rejected as too ethnic or exclusive. Buchanan Interview.
119. Board of Governors, 28 October 1977.
120. Executive, Board of Governors, 1979.
121. Ibid., 7 February 1980.
122. Board of Governors, 7 February, 25 April 1980, Executive, Board of Governors, 24 April 1980.
123. Board of Governors, 27 February 1981.
124. Board of Governors, 28 October 1983. The designer of the president's gown was Harcourts of Toronto.
125. College Council, 19 November 1979, 31 March 1981. An outline of the graduation procedures and protocol is found in College Council, Committee on Protocol, 3 February 1977.
126. *Post*, 23 June 1980.
127. Board of Governors, 26 October 1978.

128. Board of Governors, 24 October 1979, 2 February 1980.
129. *Post*, 14 May 1981.
130. Board of Governors, 30 October 1975, *Post*, 24 July 1978.
131. *Post*, 18 June 1982. Buchanan Interview.
132. Board of Governors, 26 February 1981.
133. Board of Governors, 29 October 1981.
134. Board of Governors, 25 February 1982.
135. Board of Governors, 26 February 1982.
136. Executive, Board of Governors, 20 June 1982, Board of Governors, 21 June 1982.
137. Executive, Board of Governors, 20 June 1982.
138. Board of Governors, 27 May 1982.

Chapter Five

1. At his testimonial dinner in November 1989, Reid is quoted as saying, "on occasion [I] regret that I ever made the transition from the ... life of the classroom", where he was very popular. *Post*, 13 November 1989. Dr. Reid died 24 December 2002 at the age of 76. *Post*, 27 December 2002.
2. *Post*, 19, 28 August 1983; 7 February, 6 May 1992.
3. Executive, Board of Governors, 29 January 1987.
4. Board of Governors, 21 June 1982.
5. Executive, Board of Governors, 7 December 1990.
6. *Post*, 15 May 1955.
7. Ibid.; Moore Interview.
8. *Post*, Article by Murdena Marshall, 30 May 1992.
9. College Council, 26 January 1983.
10. Ibid.
11. Board of Governors, 18 February 1983; College Council, 14 December 1984.
12. Board of Governors, 17 February 1984.
13. Board of Governors, 29 April 1983; College Council, 25 May 1983.
14. College Council, 25 May 1983.
15. Board of Governors, 28 October 1983.
16. Board of Governors, 17 February 1984.
17. College Council, 4 January 1984.
18. Ibid.
19. Board of Governors, 25 October 1985.
20. Ibid; *Post*, 19 December 1985.
21. Board of Governors. 18 February 1988, *Post*, 8 December 1988.
22. *Post*, 28 November 1988.
23. College Council, 1 March 1984.
24. Post, 18 June 1984; Board of Governors, 13 February 1986.
25. Board of Governors, 2 October 1985, *Post*, 19 February 1986.
26. Ibid.
27. Board of Governors, 13 June; 24 October, 20 November 1986.
28. Ibid.
29. Ibid., 30 November 1992.
30. Post, 2 March 1982.
31. Board of Governors, 25 April 1980.
32. *Post*, 2 March 1982.

33. Board of Governors, 24 October 1986.
34. Ibid., 3 January 1987.
35. Executive, Board of Governors, 9 April, 18 June 1987.
36. Board of Governors, 20 October 1988.
37. Ibid., 17 February 1989.
38. Executive, Board of Governors, 9 June 1988.
39. Executive, Board of Governors, 19 December 1988, 16 January, 16 February 1989.
40. Board of Governors, 7 December 1990; Executive, Board of Governors, 28 February 1991; *Post*, 6 April 1991.
41. Executive, Board of Governors (special meeting), 15 March 1991.
42. Executive, Board of Governors, 26 September 1991.
43. See pages 33.
44. *Post*, 16 September 1991.
45. See page 47 ff.
46. Board of Governors, 22 February, 26 April, 1985.
47. Executive, Board of Governors, 16 June 1985.
48. See page 103.
49. Executive, Board of Governors, 13 February 1986.
50. Board of Governors, 10 June 1988.
51. Board of Governors, (special meeting), 15 March 1991.
52. Executive, Board of Governors, 25 February 1982.
53. Board of Governors, 22 February 1985.
54. Executive, Board of Governors, 20 June 1982; Board of Governors, 18 June 1984; Executive, Board of Governors, 17 June 1985.
55. Executive, Board of Governors, 25 October 1985.
56. Executive, Board of Governors, 21 February 1985.
57. *Post*, 28 September 1985.
58. Executive, Board of Governors, 23 March 1988, Board of Governors, 22 April 1988.
59. Executive, Board of Governors, 10 April 1987.
60. Executive, Board of Governors, 24 April 1986.
61. The deficit of the Canada Games Complex for the first full year of operation was $50 thousand. Board of Governors, 8 July 1988.
62. College Council, 16 October 1981.
63. College Council, 31 March 1981.
64. Board of Governors, 26 February 1982.
65. College Council, 15 June 1982.
66. Board of Governors, 29 October 1982.
67. Board of Governors, 26 October 1984.
68. Board of Governors, 17 February, 26 October 1984; Executive, Board of Governors, 17 June 1984.
69. Executive, Board of Governors, 17 June 1984; Fewer had previously served as chair of the Sydney School Board; *Post*, 4 July 1984.
70. Dennison had been an employee since 1974. She had been appointed administrative assistant to the registrar in 1973.
71. Rosalie Courage had been development officer at St. Mary's University in Halifax for five years before coming to UCCB. Her office was in the AVTC building. Executive, Board of Governors, 24 May 1988.
72. Executive, Board of Governors, 22 June 1989.
73. *Post*, 18 June 1984. Convocation address of President Reid.
74. Statement by President Reid, *Post*, 9 May 1985.

75. *Post*, 17 June 1985. Convocation address of President Reid.
76. Executive, Board of Governors, 19 June 1983.
77. Executive, Board of Governors, 19 June 1983.
78. Executive, Board of Governors, 18 June 1984.
79. Board of Governors, 21 February 1985.
80. Board of Governors, 26 April 1985.
81. *Post*, 9 May 1985; Board of Governors, 17 June 1985.
82. Board of Governors, 25 October 1985.
83. Board of Governors, special meeting, 3 July 1986.
84. Board of Governors, 10 April 1987.
85. Board of Governors, 10 April, 19 June, 1987.
86. Executive, Board of Governors, 23 March 1988.
87. UCCB was still at the lower end of the tuition pack. Tuition for arts and science: UCCB, $1680; Dalhousie, $1680; UNB, $1775; Mt. Allison, $1830; Mt St. Vincent, $1815. Board of Governors, 8 July 1988.
88. Board of Governors, 8 July 1988.
89. Board of Governors, 8 July 1988, 4 April 1988; Memorandum, William Gallivan to University College Community, "Horizons Commission", 31 October 1988; Board of Governors, 16 January 1991.
90. Board of Governors, 28 October 1988; Executive, Board of Governors, 19 December 1988.
91. Executive, Board of Governors, 16 February 1989.
92. Executive, Board of Governors, 17 April 1989; Addlington, A.K. *A Review*.
93. Executive, Board of Governors, 19, 20 October 1989.
94. Executive, Board of Gove, 26 May 1989.
95. College Council, 8 June 1989; Board of Governors, 28 June 1989.
96. Executive, Board of Governors, 19 October 1989.
97. Gallivan Interview.
98. Board of Governors, 23 June 1989.
99. Board of Governors, 28 October 1988.
100. Board of Governors, 28 April 1989.
101. Executive, Board of Governors, 18 February 1988.
102. Interview with William Gallivan, 9 December 2003.
103. Board of Governors, 28 October 1988.
104. *Post*, 21 November 1986.

Chapter Six

1. *Post*, 18 February 1989.
2. Hill Interview.
3. Executive, Board of Governors, 19 October 1989.
4. Executive, Board of Governors, 21 October 1989.
5. Executive, Board of Governors, 21 November 1989.
6. Executive, Board of Governors, 25 January 1990. The deans, in the order the schools appear in the text, were William Wiseman, William Clemens, David White, Harvey Johnstone and Brian Seville, and Raymond Ivany. For the controversy over the role of extension (continuing education); Hill Interview.
7. First office holders of these positions were: Robert Morgan (Research), Carl "Bucky" Buchanan (Alumni), Tim Belliveau (Marketing), Kathryn Schwarek (Computer Services),

Purchasing and Human Resources vacant, Donald Fewer (Student Services) and Michelle Strenkowski (Co-op Placements).
8. Judy Head was the chief librarian. Sister Rita MacInnis Congregation of Notre Dame (1924-2000) had served in the position from 1967 to 1988, following Sister Margaret Beaton CND.
9. According to William Gallivan, despite an appearance of openness, Hill showed strong autocratic tendencies. Gallivan Interview.
10. Executive, Board of Governors, 25 January 1990.
11. The first Director of Research and Development remained in that position until 1999.
12. Peter Hill to Joel Matheson, 20 December 1989, in Board of Governors, 20 December 1989.
13. Executive, Board of Governors, 29 March 1990.
14. *Post*, 6 April 1990.
15. Board of Governors, 30 March 1990.
16. Executive, Board of Governors, 29 March 1990.
17. Board of Governors, 30 March 1990.
18. Ibid.
19. Ibid. The Computer Assisted Design/Computer Assisted Manufacturing Centre under the direction William Bugg (d.2002), had been organized at the university with a large government grant and seemed well-placed to help high-tech manufacturing in the area and to bring added revenue to the institution.
20. Executive, Board of Governors, 25 January 1990.
21. Board of Governors, 30 March 1990.
22. Board of Governors, 30 March, 27 April 1990. Hill Interview.
23. Executive, Board of Governors, 1 June 1990.
24. American-born Albrecht had held numerous staff jobs in American colleges and in the National Football League, with such teams as the Toronto Argonauts as well as the Montreal Alouettes. Buchanan's views come from his interview.
25. *Post*, 4 August 1989.
26. Buchanan Interview.
27. Gallivan Interview.
28. Executive, Board of Governors, 25 January, 29 March 1990. The $100,000 figure is disputed by Buchanan who claims the event actually lost money, since well-known names on the team had to be paid from this. Hill claimed $50,000 was raised and that Premier John Buchanan would make up the remainder. However the later lawsuit and ensuing disruptions prevented this from happening. Hill Interview.
29. Executive, Board of Governors, 7 June 1990.
30. Ibid.
31. Ibid.
32. Ibid.
33. Board of Governors, 8 June 1990.
34. Ibid.
35. Executive, Board of Governors, 7 June 1990.
36. Executive, Board of Governors, 29 June 1990.
37. *Post*, 24 August 1990.
38. Executive, Board of Governors, 29 June 1990. Hill was also absent for the executive meeting of 18 July 1990.William Gallivan warned Hill directly of the danger of his situation. Gallivan Interview.
39. Terry had taken a leave of absence for one and one-half years to become Chair of the MPHEC. His return to the administration of the University College had been opposed by

some senior members of administration. Dr. Campbell, however, had taken him back as Vice-President, Community Affairs. Terry Interview.
40. Board of Governors, 14 August 1990. Tom MacNeil was added the next day. Terry Interview.
41. Board of Governors, 14 August 1990. Members present were Joe Shannon, John Terry, Irving Schwartz, John MacPherson, Michael Mahar and Raymond MacLean.
42. Members of the committee were: Bob MacLean (Student Union president), Mike Mahar (faculty), Fred Springston (faculty), Ray MacLean, Willie Sneddon, Greg O'Keefe (all community), and John MacPherson (representative of St. F.X.).
43. *Post*, 15 August 1990.
44. *Post*, 16 August 1990.
45. Ibid.
46. Ibid.
47. Ibid.
48. Hill Interview.
49. Ibid.
50. *Post*, 27 August 1990; Executive, Board of Governors, 7 June 1990.
51. *Post*, 17 August 1990.
52. *Post*, 17 August 1990, 18 August 1990.
53. Ibid.
54. Ibid., 24 August 1990. The Boardmore Playhouse was not actually given that name until 27 September 1990; Board of Governors, 27 September 1990.
55. Board of Governors, 27 September 1990.
56. Ibid.
57. Executive, Board of Governors, 10 September 1990.
58. *Post*, 22 October 1990.
59. Board of Governors, 26 October 1990; *Post*, 22 November 1990. The committee alleged it had contacted the board three times without receiving and answer.
60. *Post*, 26, 27 November 1990.
61. Executive, Board of Governors, 20 August 1990; Board of Governors, 7 December 1990. Buchanan has indicated that parents had been flown in for the first game. Buchanan Interview.
62. Executive, Board of Governors, 7 December 1990.
63. *Post*, 31 June 1991.
64. Executive, Board of Governors, 25 October 1990; Board of Governors, 26 October 1990.
65. Executive, Board of Governors, 25 October 1990.The University College administration had previously been given authorization to borrow to a limit of $5,000,000. Executive, Board of Governors, 10 September 1990.
66. Executive, Board of Governors, 10 September 1990. and Executive, Board of Governors, 29 November 1990.
67. Executive, Board of Governors, 29 November 1990.
68. Board of Governors, 7 December 1990.
69. Ibid.
70. Executive, Board of Governors, 7 December 1990.
71. For budgetary purposes, the University College was divided into six sectors: President's Office, Research and Development, Vice-President Academic, Vice-President Administration and Finance, Library and Human Resources/Student Services. Executive, Board of Governors, 31 June 1991.
72. Board of Governors, 1 March 1991. Terry Interview.
73. Ibid., 31 January 1991.

74. Ibid., 1 March 1991.
75. Ibid., 31 January 1991.
76. Executive, Board of Governors, 4 February 1991.
77. Executive, Board of Governors, Special Meeting, 4 February 1991.
78. *Post*, 2 February 1991.
79. Executive, Board of Governors, 28 February 1991.
80. Board of Governors, 1 March 1991.
81. *Post*, 22 February 1991.
82. Board of Governors, 1 March 1991.
83. Ibid.
84. Attachment, Auditor General to John Terry, 17 September 1990, in Executive, Board of Governors, 28 February 1991.
85. Executive, Board of Governors, Special Meeting, 15 March 1991; *Post*, 22 March 1991; John Terry later confessed to being naive at the time and felt no one knew the true financial state of the institution since MacNeil had operated quite independently and had not revealed it to him. Terry Interview. William Gallivan contends that Shannon wanted MacNeil dismissed. Gallivan Interview.
86. Gallivan Interview.
87. *Post*, 20 March, 22 March 1991.
88. *Post*, 30 March 1991.
89. Board of Governors, 26 April 1991.
90. *Post*, letter to the editor, 22 March 1991.
91. Elizabeth Cooper, CA, had been trained at Touche Ross in Sydney. She had been awarded a BBA from UCCB and in 1988 won the Harry G. Haben Memorial Prize as the CA student with the highest mark in the Uniform Final Examination in the Atlantic Provinces. *Post*, 5 April 1991.
92. Executive, Board of Governors, 25 April 1991.
93. Board of Governors, 26 April 1991.
94. *Post*, 13 June 1999.
95. Executive, Board of Governors, 6 June 1991.
96. Executive, Board of Governors, 17 June 1991.
97. Ibid.
98. Executive, Board of Governors, 4 July 1991.
99. Executive, Board of Governors, 25 July 1991; *Post*, 27 July 1991.
100. *Post*, 19 August 1991; Executive, Board of Governors, 25 July 1991.
101. Executive, Board of Governors, 29 August 1991; Board of Governors, 25 October 1991.
102. Executive, Board of Governors, 29 August 1991.
103. *Post*, 22 March 1991; Board of Governors, 12 July 1991; Executive, Board of Governors, 25 October 1991.
104. Executive, Board of Governors, 25 October 1991, 25 April 1991.
105. *Post*, 20 August 1991.
106. *Post*, 15 June 1991.
107. Board of Governors, 1 March 1991.
108. *Post*, 20 March 1991.
109. Executive, Board of Governors, 25 April 1991.
110. Board of Governors, Special Meeting, 12 June 1991; *Post*, 7,8 June 1991.
111. Ibid.
112. Executive, Board of Governors, 6 June 1991.
113. *Post*, 11 June 1991.

114. *Post,* 12 June 1991.
115. *Post*, 14, 18 June 1991.
116. Executive, Board of Governors, 17 June 1991; *Post,*, 18 June 1991.
117. *Post,*, 8 June 1991; Executive, Board of Governors, 25 July 1991.
118. Executive, Board of Governors, 19 December 1988; *Post*, 19 March 1991; Gallivan Interview.
119. Executive, Board of Governors, 27 September 1990.
120. Board of Governors, 7 December 1990.
121. Executive, Board of Governors, 31 January, 28 February 1991.
122. Executive, Board of Gove, 25 July, 29 August 1991.
123. Executive, Board of Gove, 26 September 1991.
124. Board of Governors, attachment, 6 August 1991.
125. Executive, Board of Governors, 30 June 1992.
126. Board of Governors, 30 October 1992. Previous to the re-investment, the endowment fund totalled $2,400,000.
127. *Post*, 14 August 1991.
128. Board of Governors, 6 August 1991.
129. *Post*, 12,15,25, 28 October 1991.
130. *Post*, 15, 28 October 1991.
131. Criddle had been chief executive officer of the Victoria General Hospital in Halifax. Downey was currently chair of the New Brunswick Royal Commission on Excellence in Education.
132. Peat Marwick Stevenson and Kellogg, *Management Audit (*Henceforth the *Shaw-Downey Report*, 9,26.
133. *Shaw-Downey*, 14.
134. *Shaw-Downey*, 16.
135. *Shaw-Downey*, 16-18, 64-65.
136. *Shaw-Downey*, 28-29.
137. *Shaw-Downey*, 19-21.
138. *Shaw-Downey*, 43-44.
139. *Shaw-Downey*, 45-46.
140. *Shaw-Downey*, 38.
141. *Shaw-Downey*, pp. 52-53, 57.
142. *Shaw-Downey*, p. 23.
143. Interview, John Terry, 20 November 2003.
144. *Shaw-Downey*, 23-26.
145. *Shaw-Downey*, 25, 54, 64.
146. *Shaw-Downey*, 54-55.
147. *Shaw-Downey*, 62-63.
148. *Shaw-Downey*, 64.
149. *Shaw-Downey*, 34-36.
150. *Shaw-Downey*, 9, 15, 60-61, 65.
151. *Shaw-Downey*, 31-32.
152. *Shaw-Downey*, 66.
153. *Shaw-Downey*, 25.
154. *Post*, 19, 21 March 1992. Hill indicates that he had not sought tenure since it would put his successor in a difficult position. Hill Interview.
155. *Post.*
156. *Post*, 21 March 1992.
157. *Post*, 3 April 1992. Gallivan Interview.

158. *Post*, 9 April 1992.
159. *Post*, 3 April 1992. Despite his strong words, the lack of faculty support actually made Gallivan re-think his position. He called individual board members who promised their support. Like John Terry he has indicated that had he known the circumstances of the job, he would not have taken it. Gallivan Interview.
160. Gallivan Interview.
161. Gallivan Interview. This move foreshadows the later advisory committee appointed during Dr. Jacquelyn Scott's tenure.
162. *Post*, 16, 19 May 1992. See also the "Shaw Management Committee Report," 4 December 1992, attached to Peat Marwick Stevenson and Kellogg, available at the Beaton Institute.
163. Other representatives included board members John MacPherson, Clothilda Yakumchuk, Hayes MacNeil, faculty members Fred Springston, and Wayne Connors and student union president, Robert "Bobby" MacLean. *Post*, 22 May 1992.
164. Board of Governors, 25-26 June 1992.
165. *Post*, 19 August 1992.
166. Ibid.
167. Board of Governors, 30 October 1992.
168. Board of Governors, 8 June 1990.
169. Executive, Board of Governors, 27 September 1990.
170. Executive, Board of Governors, 27 September 1990.
171. Board of Governors, 26 April 1991.
172. Board of Governors, 25 October 1991, 30 November 1992, 26 February 1993; *Post*, 20 May 1992.
173. *Post*, 18 December 1992. Sadly, Gallivan's work during this trying period has never formally been recognized by the Board. He received a six-month sabbatical and his salary was lowered to that of Associate Professor. Gallivan Interview.

Chapter Seven

1. Board of Governors, 30 October 1992. Jacquelyn Thayer Scott, 47 years of age, a native of Ellsworth, Kansas, had received her MBA at the University of Manitoba and PhD in public administration from the University of Colorado in 1992. She had operated her own public relations and management consulting firm and in 1970 had won the National Newspaper Award for editorial writing. For the previous five years, she had been director of Continuing Studies at the University of Toronto, was past-president of the Ontario University Continuing Education Association and was currently president of the national association. She was the mother of three children. *Post*, 30, 31 October 1992, 29 April 1993.
2. William Gallivan, who had served as interim president, received a stipend of $9,600, equivalent to the amount received by John Terry while in that position. Board of Governors, 28 January 1993.
3. *Post*, 30, 31 October 1992. For Hill's attitude to tenure, see Chapter 6 note 154.
4. Scott Interview.
5. Ibid.; Scott, in *Post*, 17 August 1998.
6. Shaw-Downey Report, 1; Scott Interview.
7. Scott Interview.
8. *Post*, 17 August 1998.
9. Scott Interview.
10. Executive, Board of Governors, 28 January 1993.

11. Board of Governors, 24 September 1993. The board executive was composed of 12 members: a chair, vice-chair, secretary, the president, senior vice-president (position soon to be terminated), a student, and six more board members.
12. *Post*, 31 December 1992.
13. Executive, Board of Governors, 28 January 1993.
14. UCCB *Strategic Plan*, November, 1993. The work of Keith Brown and his committee in this exercise set the precedent for later such reviews.
15. Memorandum, to the University College Community, from the Strategic Planning Committee, 1 November 1993.
16. Board of Governors, 19 November 1993.
17. UCCB *Strategic Plan*, n.p.
18. Board of Governors, 28 January 1994; *Post*, 4 July 1994.
19. Board of Governors, 28 April 1994.
20. Board of Governors, 21 October 1994.
21. Executive, Board of Governors, 29 August 1991. This memo was signed by those mentioned, and Brian Conrod and Gregory MacLeod. The Shaw-Downey Report had also noted the decline in importance of the Academic Council. Shaw-Downey Report, 19-21.
22. Board of Governors, 28 April 1994. See page 136 and Chapter 6 note 137.
23. *Post*, 30 September 1993.
24. Board of Governors, 28 April, 21 October, 1994.
25. Ibid.
26. Ibid.
27. Board of Governors, 28 April 1994; *Post*, 12 October 1994.
28. *Post*, 30 September 1993.
29. Rendell had previously served at Campion College, University of Regina; Manley, a forest geneticist, and graduate of Yale University, began serving his second term, replacing Lino Polegato who had died January, 1993; Kavanagh, MBA, had taught at UCCB since 1986; Cameron, a noted author, had previously taught at universities of British Columbia and New Brunswick, as well as Dalhousie.
30. White had received his Masters of Theology at Princeton in 1969. *Post*, 1 August 1994.
31. The position of Dean of Extension was filled by Keith Brown.
32. Ivany had received his BA at the College of Cape Breton and his MS in environmental health-industrial hygiene from East Tennessee State University, studying as a Rotary International Ambassadorial Scholar. He had previously served as research fellow in the Department of Environmental Science and Physiology at the School of Public Health at Harvard University. He held diplomas in environmental engineering technology from CCB and NSEIT. He was a native of Cape Breton, having attended Reserve District High School. *Post*, 30 August 1993. Ivany later went on to become president of Nova Scotia Community College.
33. Besides the deans, other members were the chief librarian, directors of research and development, buildings and grounds, finances, public relations and human resources.
34. *Post*, 17 August 1998.
35. Ibid.
36. Though Scott was not Shannon's first choice for president, he soon showed admiration for her after he "saw a little of me," as Scott neatly puts it. Scott Interview.
37. *Post*, 8 December 1998.
38. Ibid., 6 May 1992.
39. Board of Governors, 24 October 1997.
40. Ibid., 11 October 1996; *Post*, 8 December 1998.
41. Board of Governors, 28 October 1999, 27 October 200, 19 October 2001, 27 June 2002. The 2002 preliminary estimate was for a 20 percent increase.

42. *Post*, 22 April 1992. Report by Dennis Cassivi, Program Director, Extension and Community Affairs.
43. Ibid., 17 April 1995.
44. *Post*, 17, 15 November 1997.
45. Board of Governors, 28 February 1997; *Post*, 16 December 1999.
46. Scott Interview.
47. *Post*, 16 December 1999. 3 May, 21 June 1996, 11 December 1998, 26 February, 28 October 1999.
48. *Post*, 22 September 1997.
49. Ibid., 1 November 1996.
50. Ibid., 19 January 1998; Board of Governors, 28 June 2001.
51. *Post*, 13 December 1999.
52. *Post*, 3 May, 21 June 1996, 24 April 1998.
53. *Post*, 28 August, Board of Governors, 28 October 1999.
54. *Post*, 27 January 1999.
55. Executive, Board of Governors, 28 January 1993. The name 'ATCO' refers to the name of the firm leasing the trailers.
56. Teresa MacNeil to Vince Cunningham, 26 October 1993.
57. Executive, Board of Governors, 7 June, 29 June, 20 August, 1990.
58. Board of Governors, 30 March 1990.
59. Special meeting, Executive, Board of Governors, 8 April 1993.
60. Board of Governors, 30 April 1993.
61. Ibid.
62. Ibid.
63. Special meeting, Executive, Board of Governors, 8 April 1993.
64. *Post*, 9, 10 April, 1993.
65. Ibid., 13 , 17 April, 1993.
66. Ibid.
67. Ibid., 16 April 1993.
68. Ibid., 20 May 1993.
69. *Coastal Courier*, 19 May 1993.
70. *Post*, 15 May 1993.
71. Ibid., 1 June 1993.
72. Ibid., 14 June 1993.
73. MacNeil to Cunningham, 26 October 1993.
74. "Comparison of Some Features of AVTC and UCCB Programs," attached to the above.
75. *Post*, 22 November 1993.
76. *Post*, 22, 26 November, 1993.
77. *Post*, 11 October 1995.
78. *Post*, 17 June 1996.
79. *Post*, 26 September 1991, 30 June 1992.
80. UCCB Environmental Consulting Services, January, 1993.
81. Board of Governors, 29 June, 30 October, 1992.
82. *Post*, 12 December 1994.
83. Scott Interview.
84. UCCB, President's Report, 1996-1997, 3, 1997-1998, 4.
85. Board of Governors, 21 June 1996.
86. Board of Governors, 26 February 1993.
87. *Chronicle-Herald*, 29 January 1993.
88. *Post*, 12 October 1994. The Lab is now (2003) privately incorporated.

89. *Post*, 23 November, 1996, 11 November 1997, 31 August 1998.
90. *Post*, 1 July, 15 September, 2000.
91. *Post*, 14 December 1999, 8 December 2001.
92. *Post*, 17 September 1998. Professors Katherine Covell (Psychology) and Brian Howe (Political Science) have delivered numerous papers on the rights of children, including sessions at the UN and in Geneva.
93. Early occupants of these positions were respectively Robert Campbell, soon followed by Joanne Gallivan, (for Research and Library Services) and Keith Brown (for DETI).
94. *Post*, 1 November 1996.
95. Executive, Board of Governors, 28 January 1993; Board of Governors, 30 April 1993.
96. *Post*, 13 March 1993.
97. Board of Governors, 6 April 1994. This led to the famous incident of the "Dingwall," named for federal minister David Dingwall, who was largely responsible for obtaining funding for the repairs. Part of the work included the erection of a dry stone wall along the front of the university college; some members of the community were critical of this: hence the name "Dingwall."
98. Board of Governors, 6 April 1994.
99. Board of Governors, 23 June 1995.
100. Board of Governors, 8 December 1995.
101. *Post*, 28 March, 15 November, 1995.
102. *Post*, 15 April 1996.
103. Board of Governors, 3 May 1996.
104. In 1998, there was a surplus of $75,674; in 1999, the surplus was $69,413. Board of Governors, 24 April 1998, 23 April 1999. See also the *Post*, 27 August 1997. Tuition increases at other universities, 1991-96: Mt. Allison 55%, King's (Halifax) 56%, Acadia 57%, St. Mary's and Dalhousie 63%, TUNS 83%.
105. *Post*, 27 January, 8 April, 1998.
106. Board of Governors, 24 April 1998.
107. Board of Governors, 26 June 1978.
108. *Post*, 3 September 1998. Part of the problem lay in the funding formula's relatively low rating for the University College's technology and BSc programs. As well, trades training funding was not included.
109. Board of Governors, 23 April 1999.
110. *Post*, 21 March 1992, 30 September 1993; Board of Governors, 28 April 1994. See also page 150.
111. *Post*, 30 September 1993.
112. Ibid.
113. *Post*, 17 November 1998.
114. Scott Interview.
115. *Post*, 8 June 1999.
116. The exceptions were the buildings and grounds staff and the librarians; the latter were part of the FAUT.
117. Board of Governors, 10 December 1999.
118. Board of Governors, 18 December 1999.
119. *Post*, 7 January 2000.
120. *Post*, 12 January 2000.
121. *Post*, 29 January 2000ff.
122. *Post*, 2 February 2000.
123. *Post*, 9 February 2000.
124. *Post*, 28, 29 February 2000.

125. *Post*, 23 February 2000.
126. *Post*, 2 March 2000.
127. *Post*, 3 March 2000. Scott claims to have received considerable hate mail during her term of office. Scott Interview.
128. *Post*, 12 February 2000.
129. *Post*, 10 March 2000.The mediator was Milton Veniot.
130. *Post*, 17 March 2000.
131. The union had sought a 30-percent increase; UCCB had earlier offered a 16-percent increase over five years.
132. *Post*, 10-18 April 2000.
133. *Post*, 18 March 2000.
134. *Post*, 14 June 2000.
135. *Post*, 30 June 2000.
136. *Post*, 11 November 1994.
137. *Post*, 19 November 1998.
138. See page 174.
139. Board of Governors, 29 June 2000.
140. Board of Governors, 21 March 2000.
141. Board of Governors, 4 May 2000.
142. Board of Governors, 28 June 2001.
143. Board of Governors, 19 October 2001.
144. *Post*, 20 October 2001.
145. Board of Governors, 15 March 2002.
146. *Post*, 6 March 2002.
147. *Post*, 15 March 2002.
148. *Post*, 16 March 2002.
149. Ibid.
150. *Post*, 20 March 2002.
151. Board of Governors, 26 April 2002.
152. Board of Governors, 14 May 2002.

Bibliography

All items mentioned in this bibliography are available at the Beaton Institute unless otherwise indicated.

Newspapers

Cape Breton Post, 1955-2003.
The Casket, 8 December 1966.
Chronicle Herald, 1962, et seriatim.
Coastal Courier, May, 1993.
Excalibur [*Xcalibur*], 1965, 1970.
Highlander, November 1968, December 1970, February 1971.
Post Record, 1951, 1952.
Spokesman (St. F. X.), vol.1, #3, [fall, 1966].
Sydney Daily Post, 1905.
Sydney Post, 1922.
Sydney Post-Record, 1947.
Xaverian Weekly, 1966, 1973.

Abbreviation

Post *Cape Breton Post*, 1955-2003
Post Record, 1951, 1952
Sydney Daily Post, 1905
Sydney Post, 1922
Sydney Post-Record, 1947

Unpublished Sources:

Manuscripts

Boyle, Rev. Thomas O. Papers. MG 13,166.
Butts, Sr. Peggy. Papers. MG 13, 47.
Campbell, D.F. Papers. MG 11, 56.
Canadian Association of University Teachers. Papers. MG 11, 33.
College of Cape Breton. College Council Papers, 1974. MG 1,1.
Doucet, A.A. *College for Cape Breton*. 1937. In MG 13, 53, 3 a.
Hogan, Rev. Andrew. Papers. MG 9, 47, 3 c.
Huntjens, Jan. Papers. MG 12 , 57.
MacDonald, William. Papers. MG 12, 88.
MacLellan, M.A. Journal, 1951. MG 13, 59.
———. *Xavier Junior College, 1951-1964*, . MG 13, 2d.
MacLeod, Rev. Gregory. Papers. MG 11, 44, 10.
Morgan, R.J. Papers. MG 12, 82.

Morrison, D.S. Papers. MG 12, 46.
Nicholson, John J. "St. FX has a Soul." MG 1,1, A 13, file 1a.
Saint Francis Xavier University, Board of Governors. Minutes, 1951-1974. MG 1, 1, A2.
———. Executive Minutes, 1974-1975.
———. Senate Minutes, 1970-1974. MG 1, A1, files 89-91.
Tompkins, Rev. J.J. Papers MG 10, 2.
University College of Cape Breton. Correspondence, memoranda, reports pertaining to the College of Cape Breton and its antecedents. MG 1, 1.
———. Academic Council Papers, 1976-1981.
———. Board of Governors Minutes, 1973-2002. MG 1, 1 A1. Minutes dating from 1983 onward are available only at Board of Governors' office.
———. Centre for International Studies. MG 1, 10.
———. Drama. MG 15, 30.
———. Executive Committee Minutes, Board of Governors, 1974-1993. Minutes after 1993 are not open.
———. Office of the President, MG 1, 1A, 2.

Interviews by the author

Buchanan, Carl "Bucky," 25 January 2004.
Cunningham, Vincent, 8 December 2003.
Hill, Dr. Peter, 11 January 2004.
Gallivan, William, 9 December 2003.
MacLeod, Rev. Gregory, 29 December 2003.
Scott, Dr. Jacquelyn, 17 December 2003.
Terry, John, 20 November 2003.

Informational sessions were also held with Rev. D.F. Campbell, Steven Kavanagh and the late T.L. Sullivan.

Taped Sessions

Strategic Planning [1994]. Six audio tapes regarding enrollment data, research, student role and responsibilities, teaching, and learning and scholarship. T-3188, T-3189, T-3190.

Unpublished Reports

Addlington, A.K. *A Review of the [Maritime Provinces Higher Education] Commission's Funding Formula.* A.K. Addlington to Finance Committee, MPHEC, 1 December 1988. In Executive Minutes, Board of Governors, 19 December 1988.
Anonymous. *Chronological Development of the Xavier College Question*. [1963-1973].
Anonymous. *UCCB, A Brief History*, n.d.
Anonymous. *UCCB Funding Formula. Where we are and how we got there*, 1998.

Arseneau, Catherine. *The Founding of Xavier Junior College.* 10 April 1990. Reports: Education.

Campbell, D.F. *An Idea Whose Time Had Come.* In Board of Governors, 22 October 1971.

———. *What's In a Name?* Reports: Education.

Facts About Xavier [1964]. MG 1, 1, A2a, file 18.

Lyceum Restoration. n.d. Reports: Museums.

MacLellan, Malcolm A. *The Importance of Conservatism in Education.* M.A thesis, June 1933.

MacLeod, Donald. *Birth of a University*, n.d.

Stevens, Francis. *Xavier College Library - History September 1951 - July 1967*, n.d.

UCCB. *Strategic Plan*, November 1993. Not yet catalogued.

———. *Report presented to the College Council by the Objectives Committee*, 1980.

Maps, Views, and Plans

College of Cape Breton Campus. Artist's Conception of new CCB Campus, 1975. Leaflet 945.

———. Plans for New Building. 1978. Roll Map 7.

Colour slides of the institution and its activities are available at the Beaton Institute. Slides Collection, boxes 1-12.

UCCB. *Residence Project*, 1980.

Woodcock and Associates Ltd. *Master Plan - report for the site developments, services and buildings for new post-secondary educational facilities at Cape Breton*, 1974.

Scrapbooks

UCCB (and antecedents) Scrapbooks, 1951 - 2000.

———. Directories, Scrapbook 163, 1976-80.

Bibliography

Boyle, George. *Father Tompkins of Nova Scotia.* New York: P.J. Kenedy, 1953.

Boyle, Thomas. *Justice Through Power.* Toronto: Longmans, 1961.

Bras d'Or Institute. "A Study of Enrollment Potentials, 1977-1987." Technical Bulletin #5, May 1977.

———. "UCCB and the Community." 3 August 1988.

Brunell, Yves, " A Centenarian's Progeny Makes Good." *Cape Breton Mirror.* 1, #8, 23.

Cameron, James D. *For The People, a History of St. Francis Xavier University.* Montreal: McGill-Queen's University Press, 1996.

Coady, Moses M. *Masters of Their Own Destiny*. New York: Harper, 1939.

Donovan, Kenneth. "May Learning Flourish," in *The Island. New Perspectives on Cape Breton History, 1713-1990. Acadiensis Press, UCCB Press, 1990.*

Higgins, Benjamin. *Cape Breton And Its University College: Symbiotic Development.* Sydney, NS: UCCB Press, 1994.

Johnston, A.A. *History of the Catholic Church in Eastern Nova Scotia.* St. Francis Xavier University: Hunter Rose, 1958.

Lauwreys, Joseph A., *Final Report, Submitted To the Committee Appointed By the Premier to Study Post-Secondary Education In Cape Breton.*
Nearing, Peter. *He Loved The Church.* Antigonish: Casket Printing, 1975.
Nova Scotia. Laws of Nova Scotia. Chapter 4, 23 Eliz. II. *An Act To Establish the College Of Cape Breton And Incorporate Its Board Of Governors*, 1974.
———. Statutes of Nova Scotia. *An Act To Change The Name Of The College Of Cape Breton And To Amend Chapter 4, Of The Act Of 1974, An Act To Establish The College Of Cape Breton And Incorporate Its Board Of Governors*, 1982.
Patterson, Paul and Susan Biagi. *The Loom of Change: Weaving a New Economy on Cape Breton.* Sydney, NS: UCCB Press, 2003
Peat Marwick Stevenson and Kellogg. *Management Audit and General Examination of All Aspects of the Operations of the University College of Cape Breton.* [Shaw-Downey report], 19 March 1992.
Pope, William, ed. *Clarence MacKinnon Nicholson.* Hantsport: Lancelot Press, 1981.
Recommendations of the Special Committee appointed by Premier Regan to present a plan for Post-secondary Education in Cape Breton, [1973].
Taylor, Leiberfeld and Heldman (Canada). *Report to St. Francis University, An Analysis of Prospective Growth and Development Patterns*, January 1979.
———. *A Physical Plant Development Program for Xavier College.* March, 1967. MG 1, 1, A20, file 2a.
University College of Cape Breton and antecedents. Calendars, 1951-2002.
———. Environmental Consulting Services, January, 1993.

INDEX